T0301787

MANAGEMENT OF SERVICE BUSINESSES IN JAPAN

Japanese Management and International Studies
(ISSN: 2010-4448)

Editor-in-Chief: Yasuhiro Monden *(Tsukuba University, Japan)*

Published

Vol. 1   Value-Based Management of the Rising Sun
*edited by Yasuhiro Monden, Kanji Miyamoto, Kazuki Hamada,
Gunyung Lee & Takayuki Asada*

Vol. 2   Japanese Management Accounting Today
*edited by Yasuhiro Monden, Masanobu Kosuga,
Yoshiyuki Nagasaka, Shufuku Hiraoka & Noriko Hoshi*

Vol. 3   Japanese Project Management:
KPM — Innovation, Development and Improvement
edited by Shigenobu Ohara & Takayuki Asada

Vol. 4   International Management Accounting in Japan:
Current Status of Electronics Companies
edited by Kanji Miyamoto

Vol. 5   Business Process Management of Japanese and Korean Companies
*edited by Gunyung Lee, Masanobu Kosuga, Yoshiyuki Nagasaka &
Byungkyu Sohn*

Vol. 6   M&A for Value Creation in Japan
edited by Yasuyoshi Kurokawa

Vol. 7   Business Group Management in Japan
edited by Kazuki Hamada

Vol. 8   Management of an Inter-Firm Network
edited by Yasuhiro Monden

Vol. 9   Management of Service Businesses in Japan
*edited by Yasuhiro Monden, Noriyuki Imai, Takami Matsuo &
Naoya Yamaguchi*

Japanese Management and International Studies – Vol. 9

MANAGEMENT OF SERVICE BUSINESSES IN JAPAN

editors

Yasuhiro Monden
Tsukuba University, Japan

Noriyuki Imai
Toyota Financial Services Corporation, Japan

Takami Matsuo
Kobe University, Japan

Naoya Yamaguchi
Niigata University, Japan

 **World Scientific**

NEW JERSEY · LONDON · SINGAPORE · BEIJING · SHANGHAI · HONG KONG · TAIPEI · CHENNAI

Published by

World Scientific Publishing Co. Pte. Ltd.

5 Toh Tuck Link, Singapore 596224

USA office: 27 Warren Street, Suite 401-402, Hackensack, NJ 07601

UK office: 57 Shelton Street, Covent Garden, London WC2H 9HE

Library of Congress Cataloging-in-Publication Data
Management of service businesses in Japan / editors, Yasuhiro Monden ... [et al.].
    p. cm. -- (Japanese management and international studies, ISSN 2010-4448 ; v. 9)
    Includes bibliographical references and index.
    ISBN 978-9814374668 (alk. paper)
    1. Service industries--Japan--Management. 2. Industrial management--Japan
I. Monden, Yasuhiro, 1940–
    HD9987.J32M36 2013
    658.00952--dc23

                        2012035819

British Library Cataloguing-in-Publication Data
A catalogue record for this book is available from the British Library.

In-house Editor: DONG Lixi

Typeset by Stallion Press
Email: enquiries@stallionpress.com

Printed in Singapore.

Japan Society of Organization and Accounting (JSOA)

Mission of JSOA and Editorial Information

For the purpose of making a contribution to the business and academic communities, the Japan Society of Organization and Accounting (JSOA), is committed to publishing the book series, entitled *Japanese Management and International Studies*, with a refereed system.

Focusing on Japan and Japan-related issues, the series is designed to inform the world about research outcomes of the new "Japanese-style management system" developed in Japan. However, as the series title suggests, it also promotes *"International Studies"* on the interface of managerial competencies between Japan and other countries that include Asian countries as well as Western countries under the globalized business activities of Japanese companies.

Research topics included in this series are management of organizations in a broad sense (including the business group or networks) and the accounting that supports the organization. More specifically, topics include business strategy, business models, organizational restoration, corporate finance, M&A, environmental management, operations management, managerial & financial accounting, manager performance evaluation, reward systems. The research approach is interdisciplinary, which includes case studies, theoretical studies, normative studies and empirical studies, but emphasizes real world business.

Each volume contains the series title and a book title which reflects the volume's special theme.

Our JSOA's board of directors has established an editorial board of international standing. In each volume, guest editors who are experts on the volume's special theme serve as the volume editors.

Editorial Board

Contents

Preface

Contemporary competition among firms has become competition among the inter-firm networks. Therefore, it is insufficient for only one company to stand out, for instance, we can not just have manufacturing plants high in their productivity, quality and costs, etc. Rather all participating companies in the network, from research & development, production engineering, manufacturing, general strategic decision & control, to logistics, distribution & sales, finance, after-services and so on, must all show their core competence in its own function in the value chain. In other words, the cost, quality and productivity (e.g. lead-time and flexibility, etc.) of non-manufacturing industries must all be good and eventually perform good figures in their bottom line, so that the inter-firm network as a whole could be competitive among inter-network competition. Here is the necessity of improving the productivity of non-manufacturing industries and the need for bench-marking the better know-how of various service businesses.

When it comes to referring to the term "service" in this volume, we don't merely grasp it as the "service industry" that belongs to the third industry, but also includes the services of the public sectors and NPO (non-profit organizations), whose cases of their services' improvements are introduced.

Further the concept of the "performance improvement" of services in this volume is rather broad, and it can be rephrased as "performance management" in the general management theory. Therefore, it doesn't confine to the lead-time reduction and the inventory reduction, etc. but it includes all of the performance control policies covering the service quality improvement, sales revenue enhancement, cost reduction, and profit enlargement and so forth of the service businesses.

So far there has not so many that disclosed the Japanese ways of performance improvement in the service industries in a broad sense. However, there are many unique Japanese approaches for this topic. All chapters in this book are based on concrete case studies and derived useful propositions, thus applicable to service businesses in general. Unique treatment of topics includes:

PART 1: Advanced Service Management in the Service Industries

The world's No.1 know-how of the convenience store chain of Seven-Eleven in Japan, the sales finance and auto sales business of Toyota Motors, and application of Toyota production system to insurance companies were examined.

PART 2: Advanced Service Management in the Public and Non-Profit Organizations

Further the performance management system of Japanese local governments, the balance scorecard in Japanese hospitals, and the pricing of Telecommunication Company were discussed.

PART 3: General Concepts and Techniques Applied to the Service Management

Especially interesting and useful is Japanese-like "hospitality" in the retail and hotel businesses, the service level agreement (SLA) in IT companies, and IT applied to BPN (Business Process Network) of service industry.

We hope that it will be meaningful to transmit such case-based know-how to the overseas.

Acknowledgements

I am very grateful to Ms. Juliet Lee Ley Chin, the senior commissioning editor of the Social Sciences in the World Scientific Publishing Company for her invaluable advice to make this volume a reality. Further, Ms. Tang Yu and Ms. Dong Lixi, the desk editors, are acknowledged for their handling the manuscripts. The contributing authors of this volume are also amply rewarded when their new ideas or knowledge contribute to the literature on business management and managerial accounting, thereby being of some use to people around the world.

Yasuhiro Monden
Principal Volume Editor
July 14, 2012

About the Editors

Yasuhiro Monden
Professor Emeritus of Tsukuba University, Japan
Visiting professor, Global Leader MBA, Nagoya University of Commerce
and Business.
Ph.D. in Management Science and Engineering from Tsukuba University
pmx00170@mail2.accsnet.ne.jp

Main Publications
Toyota Production SysteM, 4th Edition, New York: CRC Press of Tailor &
Francis Group, 2012. (The first edition was awarded the 1984 *Nikkei Prize*
by Japan Center for Economic Research and Nikkei Inc. and now recognized
as a JIT classic.)
From Adam Smith's Division of Labor to Network Organization: From the
Market Price Mechanism to the Incentive Price Mechanism, in Monden,
Y. (ed.) *Management of Inter-Firm Network*, Singapore: World Scientific
Publishing Co., 3–30 (2012).
Concept of Incentive Price for Motivating the Performance of Japanese
Firms, in Hamada, K.(ed.) *Business Group Management in Japan*, Singa-
pore: World Scientific Publishing Co., 193–208 (2010).
Profit Allocation Price for Motivating the Inter-Firm Cooperation,
Zeimukeiri Kyokai, 2009 (in Japanese).

Noriyuki Imai
Visiting Professor, Meijo University, Japan
Ph. D. from Meijo University
silverstone@mta.biglobe.ne.jp

Main Publications
*A Primer on Just-in-Time Management: From 5S to Headquarters,
Accounting and Capital market*, Tokyo, Chuokeizai-sha, Inc., 2011 (in
Japanese).
The Proposal of Dual-mode Management Accounting Model: Aiming at the
Dissolution of "Accounting Lag", *The Meijo Review*, Vol. 10, No. 4, 61–87
(2010) (in Japanese).

The Proposal of Life Cycle Costing Subsuming Time Cost of Capital Employed: A Study of the Advancement of Dual-mode Management Accounting Model," *The Meijo Review*, Vol. 11, No. 4, 131–153 (2011) (in Japanese).
"Dual-mode Management Accounting" and Capital Market: A Study of the Integration of Mid- to Long-term and Short-term Schemas," *The Meijo Review*, Vol. 12, No. 4, 17–35 (2012) (in Japanese).

Takami Matsuo
Professor, Graduate School of Business Administration, Kobe University, Japan
DBA from Kobe University
mats@kobe-u.ac.jp

Main Publications
Performance Evaluation System of Local Government, Tokyo, Chuou Keizaisha Inc., (2009) (in Japanese).
A Case Study of the Relative Performance Evaluation in Budgeting Process of Japanese Local Government, *The Kokumin-keizai Zasshi* (*Journal of Economics & Business Administration*), Vol. 205, No. 5, 53–67 (2012) (in Japanese).
Trends and Issues of Performance Evaluation Systems in Local Governments, *Sangyo Keiri*, Vol. 71, No. 4, 72–89 (2012) (in Japanese).
The Diversity and Effectiveness of Performance Evaluation Systems in Local Governments, *The Kokumin-keizai Zasshi* (*Journal of Economics & Business Administration*), Vol. 202, No. 2, 29–45 (2010) (in Japanese).
An Empirical Study on the Effectiveness of Performance Evaluation in Japanese Local Government, *Kokaikei Kenkyu*, Vol. 10, No. 1, 37–56 (2008) (in Japanese).

Naoya Yamaguchi
Associate Professor, Graduate School of Modern Society and Culture, Faculty of Economics, Niigata University, Japan
MBA from Hokkaido University
naoya@econ.niigata-u.ac.jp

Main Publications
Business Process Management of Horizontal Division Networks Created by Companies Specializing in Element Technology: Based on an Analysis

of *Polishers' Syndicate* in Tsubame, *Journal of Cost Accounting Research* (Japan Cost Accounting Association), Vol. 35, No. 1, 96–106 (2011) (in Japanese).

Inter-firm Business Process Management of Companies Specializing in Element Technology: Analysis of a Horizontal Division Network Created by a Cluster of Small Enterprises in Japan, Monden, Y. (ed.), *Management of an Inter-Firm Network*, World Scientific Publishing Co., 2011.

Current Status of Process Management in Japanese and Korean Companies, coauthored with K. Sakate, in G. K. Lee, M. Kosuga, Y. Nagasaka and B. Sohn (eds.), *Business Process Management of Japanese and Korean Companies*, World Scientific Publishing Co., 2010.

Introduction of Balanced Scorecard to Prefecture Governmental Hospitals: A Case of Niigata Prefecture Governmental Hospitals, *Government Auditing Review* (Board of Audit of Japan), Vol. 42, 107–124 (2010) (in Japanese).

Functions and Design of Performance Measurement Systems for Local Government of Japan, *Government Auditing Review* (Board of Audit of Japan), Vol. 38, 75–85 (2008) (in Japanese).

Decision Making Theory of PFI (Private Finance Initiative), Hiroshima-city, Keisuisya, 2006 (in Japanese).

List of Contributors

Akimichi Aoki
Professor, School of Business Administration, Senshu University, Japan
2-1-1 Higashimita, Tama-ku, Kawasaki-shi, Kanagawa 214-8580, Japan
MBA from Senshu University
aaoki@isc.senshu-u.ac.jp

Shino Hiiragi
Project Research Associate, Manufacturing Management Research Center,
Graduate School of Economics, University of Tokyo, Japan
7-3-1 Hongo, Bunkyo-ku, Tokyo, 113-0033, Japan
Ph.D. from Aichi Institute of Technology
s_hiiragi@nifty.com

Noriko Hoshi
Professor, Faculty of Business Management, Hakuoh University, Japan
1117 Daigyoji, Oyama City, Tochigi Prefecture 323-8585, Japan
Ph.D. from Tsukuba University
hoshi@fc.hakuoh.ac.jp

Nobuhiro Ikeda
Professor, Faculty of Management, Otemon Gakuin University, Japan
2-1-15 Nishiai Ibaraki, Osaka 567-8502, Japan
MBA from Kobe University
noikeda@res.otemon.ac.jp

Noriyuki Imai
Visiting Professor, Meijo University, Japan
1-501 Shiogamaguchi, Tenpaku-ku, Nagoya, 468-8502, Japan
Ph.D. from Meijo University
silverstone@mta.biglobe.ne.jp

Shang-Jen Li
Assistant Professor, Dept. of Hospitality Management,
  Meiho University, Taiwan
23, Pingguang Rd., Neipu, Pingtung, 91202, Taiwan, R.O.C.
Ph.D. from National Sun Yat-Sen University, Taiwan
x00010180@meiho.edu.tw

Anders W Johansson
Professor, School of Management and Economics,
  Linnaeus University, Sweden
SE-351 95 Växjö, Sweden
Ph.D. from Lund University, Sweden
anders.w.johansson@lnu.se

Gunyung Lee
Professor, Faculty of Economics, Niigata University, Japan
8050 Ikarashi 2-no-cho, Nishi-ku, Niigata, 950-2181, Japan
Ph.D. from Tsukuba University
lee@econ.niigata-u.ac.jp

Takami Matsuo
Professor, Graduate School of Business Administration,
  Kobe University, Japan
2-1 Rokkodai, Nada, Kobe 657-8501, Japan
DBA from Kobe University
mats@kobe-u.ac.jp

Yasuhiro Monden
Professor Emeritus of Tsukuba University, Japan
4-31-1 Nakaochiai, Shinjuku-ku, Tokyo 161-8539, Japan
Ph.D. in Management Science and Engineering from Tsukuba University
pmx00170@mail2.accsnet.ne.jp

Yoshiyuki Nagasaka
Professor, School of Management, Konan University, Japan
8-9-1 Okamoto, Higasinada, Kobe, 658-8501, Japan
Dr. Eng. from Osaka University
nagasaka@konan-u.ac.jp

Tomoaki Sonoda
Professor, Faculty of Business and Commerce, Keio University, Japan
2-15-45 Mita, Minato-ku, Tokyo 108-8345, Japan
Ph.D. from Keio University
sonoda@fbc.keio.ac.jp

Manabu Takano
Associate Professor, Department of Commerce, Seinan Gakuin University,
    Japan
6-2-92 Nishijin, Sawara-ku, Fukuoka 814-8511, Japan
Ph.D. from Meiji University
m-takano@seinan-gu.ac.jp

Dun-Hou Tsai
Professor, Dept. of Business Management, National Sun Yat-sen
    University, Taiwan
No. 70, Lienhai Rd., Kaohsiung 80424, Taiwan, R.O.C.
Ph.D. from National Chengchi University, Taiwan
dhtsai@bm.nsysu.edu.tw

Naoya Yamaguchi
Associate Professor, Graduate School of Modern Society and Culture
Faculty of Economics, Niigata University, Japan
8050 Ikarashi 2-no-cho, Nishi-ku, Niigata 950-2181, Japan
MBA from Hokkaido University
naoya@econ.niigata-u.ac.jp

PART 1

Advanced Service Management in the Service Industries

1

Profit Sharing that Motivates Inter-Firm Cooperation within a Convenience Store Chain

Yasuhiro Monden
University of Tsukuba

Noriko Hoshi
Hakuoh University

1 Purpose of the Study

In an inter-firm network that consists of a franchiser and so many franchisees, profit sharing is something that requires much consideration if cooperation between the two parties is to be encouraged. The author has long been exploring the concept of the "incentive price" (i.e. price for profit allocation) and its application to the members of inter-firm network for motivating their cooperation, through a series of papers of Monden (2009a; 2009b; 2010; 2012) and Monden and Nagao (1987–1988). As one of similar courses of research, Mouritsen and Thrane (2006) also advocated that the profit allocation function as a "self-regulation mechanism" by transfer prices, taxes and fees would coordinate the relationships among member firms of network. This theme is also the basic focus of the study. In this chapter, this focus is maintained as we examine various types of profit sharing structures that would motivate participation and cooperation on the part of the franchiser of a convenience-store chain and its franchisees. We would like to verify the correlations among the items listed below, in considering profit sharing.

(1) Differences in terms, when investing in or leasing store property
(2) Differences in royalty rates, from company to company
(3) Sharing the risk of disposal loss

(4) Differences in franchise fees, from company to company
(5) Sharing the risk of profit-earning among stores
(6) Sharing the cost for interior finishing work
(7) Sharing the cost of utilities

However, in this analysis, we do not consider factors such as the large amounts of initial investment made by the franchiser, operational costs, direct financing by the franchiser, or loan guarantees upon opening the store. In this chapter, we would like to construct a general proposition through analysis, by focusing on the case of Seven-Eleven Japan Co., Ltd. (hereafter abbreviated as SEJ), the most well known of all convenience store chains, and by examining complementary data from other chains.

2   Different types of Franchisees Based on the Amount of Initial Investment

First, we would like to classify franchisees into categories, based on the amount of initial investment made upon opening the store (Fig. 1).

The word "owner", used in the sense of "owner of franchisee's store" on the right-hand-side of Fig. 1, does not denote that the person is the owner of the store property as listed in the register book; it means that **the person is the store manager and owns more than 50% of the amount of investment made in the store.** In other words, the store manager has invested his or her own funds, and those funds represent the

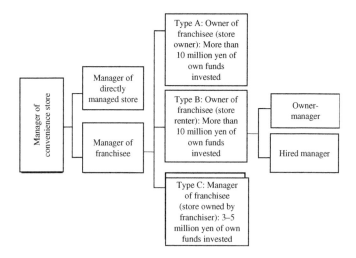

Fig. 1.   Classification of convenience store managers.

majority of fund sourcing, shown as the owners' equity in the balance sheet of the store. Therefore, a Type B franchisee — who rents store property and pays rent — is associated with this type of owner.

3 Differences in Royalty Rates Dependent on the Amount of Initial Investment

A convenience store manager assigned a store prepared by the franchiser need only bear the cost of interior finishing work as the initial cost; this means that, for the manager, the risk of not recovering his or her initial investment is very low. However, "low risk" comes "low returns" (i.e., low revenues). On the other hand, in cases where the owner-manager bears the initial investment, which incurs a "high risk", there should be "high returns" (i.e., high revenues).

According to the degree of risk by the amount of initial investment, an "owner of a franchisee store" — as we refer to him or her here — is charged a low royalty rate, whereas a "manager of a franchisee store" is charged a high royalty rate. Therefore, the "income" (i.e., gross profits on sales minus royalty) received by the store manager would be relatively high in the former case, and relatively low in the latter.

Type A (Franchisee candidate owns land and building)
The royalty charged by SEJ (called as "Seven-Eleven charge") is 43% of the gross profit on sales. However, after a period of five years or following the renewal of a 15-year contract, the rate may decrease, according to the terms in each case.[1]

Type C (Franchisee candidate with land and building provided by franchiser)
With this type, the franchiser prepares land and arranges for the building of the store; the franchisee need not even pay rent for the property.

---

[1] The rates of the other chains are as follows: (1) Lawson: 34% of total gross profit; (2) FamilyMart: 35% of gross operating profit, but if the franchiser bears a part of the cost of interior finishing work, that figure is 38%; (3) Circle K Sunkus: royalty rate versus gross profit on sales depends on the monthly gross profit on sales: 30% of gross profits on sales less than 6 million yen, 19% for 6 million and over but less than 7.5 million yen, and 14% for 7.5 million yen and over; and (4) Ministop: 30% of gross profit on sales. Most of the franchisers adopt a fixed rate for Type A ("high risk, high return"); the exception is Circle K Sunkus which uses a sliding-scale rate system.

In the case of SEJ, since the franchiser pays rent for the land and building, the royalty charged would naturally be higher than with Type A. The rate would increase on a sliding scale according to the gross profit on sales: 56% for gross profit on sales up to 2.5 million yen, 66% for over 2.5 million yen and up to 4 million yen, 71% for over 4 million yen and up to 5.5 million yen, and 76% for over 5.5 million yen (see Sakakibara, 2010, p. 14). However, after a period of 5 years or following the renewal of a 15-year contract, among other cases, the rate charged may decrease according to the terms of each case.[2] Thus, Type C is a business with low risk and low return.

Type B (*Franchisee candidate rents store space on his or her own, under his or her own name*)

This is a contract type that each of Circle K Sunkus, Ministop, and Daily Yamazaki has adopted, but others have not. Thus, this type is a rather special case.

In most cases, the franchisee itself becomes a tenant in apartment buildings, commercial buildings, and shopping malls. Renting a space costs approximately 10–15 million yen, in the form of costs such as the initial deposit, the guarantee payment, interior finishing work, and various fees. Even when renting a store space, property tenancy usually requires considerable initial investment; this includes not only the rent, but also key money and a considerable amount of guarantee payment (deposit) to the renter, as well as commissions to the real estate agent.

Since the royalty rate of Type B is the same as that charged for Type A above, the income of the store is high. At the same time, however, owing to

---

[2]The rates of the other chains are as follows: (1) Lawson: 50% of total gross profit, but if two months of average monthly sales is required as an operational security deposit, that figure is reduced to 45%; (2) FamilyMart: if franchisee bears the cost of interior finishing work, 48% of gross operating profit; if franchiser prepares everything, 48% of gross operating profit up to 3 million yen, 60% for over 3 million but less than 4.5 million yen, and 65% for over 4.5 million yen; (3) Circle K Sunkus: 37% for gross profit on sales less than 2.4 million yen, 57% for 2.4 million and over but less than 3.4 million yen, and 62% for 3.4 million yen and over; (4) Ministop: if franchisee bears the cost of interior and exterior finishing work, 36% of gross profit on sales up to 3.6 million yen, and 58% for over 3.6 million yen; if franchiser bears the cost of interior and exterior finishing work, 36% of gross profit on sales up to 3.6 million yen, 70% for over 3.6 million but less than 4.5 million yen, and 73% for over 4.5 million yen. Lawson is the only chain that adopts a fixed rate for Type C franchises; other chains adopt a sliding scale rate system.

the contract period with the franchiser (i.e., 7–10 years) or the lease contract with the store property owner, the franchisee cannot easily withdraw from the business, even when faced with sluggish sales. These conditions suggest that this type of business is also "high risk, high return", just like Type A.

There are also cases in which a franchiser would prepare the store property or rent a space and pay the rent. Again, however, the royalty rate is the same as that charged for Type A, which means that the business is both "high risk" and "high return".

4   Relationship between Royalty Rates and Break-Even Point

Before becoming a franchisee of a certain chain, those who are considering becoming a franchisee of a convenience store chain need to compare the terms of each chain in order to make an advisable buying decision. In this sense, the principle of market competition would play a role among the chains before a prospective franchisee chooses a certain chain, and the principle of market price would influence royalty, sharing, and other kinds of rates.

At this point, it is quite difficult to choose which chain would be the best investment among the many convenience store chains. Takeuchi (2001, p. 227) describes the elements inherent in the decision-making process as follows: "In the case of major chains with a large number of stores, we can expect to see a store with high daily sales (amount of sales per day), but on the flipside, the royalty is high and the benefit in terms of revenue would be low. On the other hand, in the case of chains going in a direction different from the major chains, such as Daily Yamazaki, Circle K Sunkus, Ministop, and am/pm, daily sales might be low but the royalty rate would also be low, thus resulting in high profit margin."

In this respect, the following is our perspective vis-à-vis the relationship between royalty rates and the break-even point. Since chains with higher average daily sales or higher average annual sales charge higher royalty rates, the "gross profit after loyalty" of the convenience store (= [gross profit on sales − royalty] = [sales volume − cost of goods sold − royalty] = [sales volume − total variable cost]) would be relatively low. Assuming that the fixed costs are identical across all stores, then:

$$\text{``gross profit after loyalty''}/\text{sales volume}$$
$$= \text{contribution margin ratio}$$

According to this formula, chains with higher annual sales per store would have a relatively lower contribution margin ratio. As a result, the "break-even point", calculated as the fixed cost/contribution margin ratio, should be relatively high. Therefore, a store would need to achieve considerable sales volumes to run into the black. On the other hand, since chains with small annual sales would have low royalty rates, the "contribution margin ratio" of the above would be relatively high, and the break-even point would be relatively low. Therefore, the store would be able to run into the black even with relatively low sales volumes.

5 Method of Calculating Royalty and Bearing the Cost of Disposal Loss, and Sharing the Risk of Disposal Loss

5.1 *Is a system in which the store owner bears the full disposal loss socially just?*

As long as the store is responsible for ordering stock, the store owner is of course responsible for bearing "disposal losses". However, we believe it socially unfair for the store owner to bear the full risk of disposal loss, given that, in reality, the occurrence of disposal loss is significantly dependent on the strategies of the franchiser. Franchisers say "avoid opportunity loss" (in other words, lost sales opportunities as a result of being out of stock on certain items) and alert their franchisees to follow through with an active ordering strategy. If franchisees place large orders according to this strategy set by the franchiser, the risk of generating a "disposal loss" would naturally increase. Therefore, we consider it problematic to hold franchisees entirely responsible for disposal losses and have them fully bear the risk thereof. Additionally, if the sales volume of a franchisee increases by producing a disposal loss, then the commission received by the franchiser would increase. Clearly, a system in which franchisees must bear the risk of disposal loss while franchisees receive profits from large orders is not balanced.

Ryuichi Isaka, President of SEJ, was quoted as saying that "If franchisees are worried about disposal loss and hold off placing orders, we would not be able to provide enough items (to the customers)" (*The Nikkei*, June 24, 2009). This statement suggests that the franchiser places more emphasis on avoiding "out-of-stock loss" than on avoiding "disposal loss". If this were the case, what incentive should a franchiser offer its franchisees, to encourage them to "provide enough items", without worrying about the risk of disposal loss? The answer is for the franchiser and franchisee to share the risk of disposal loss.

On June 22, 2009, the Japan Fair Trade Commission ordered SEJ to stop limiting discounts. The following day, SEJ announced that "the franchiser would bear a part (15%) of the disposal loss" (*The Nikkei*, June 24, 2009). This quick measure of compromise by SEJ had also been influenced by a new strategy called "1-yen disposal" ("1-yen sales", to be exact) by the franchisees, which involves a store discounting an item to 1 yen instead of disposing of it, and the owner of the store buying it (i.e., sales at 1 yen). This is virtually a disposed item, but it is sold, not disposed, and therefore it is recorded as 1 yen of "sales" per item sold. "The cost of goods sold" would be recorded as the cost of goods purchased; if, for instance, the item had been purchased at 100 yen, it would then be recorded as a 100-yen cost of sales, and the gross profit on sales would be "−99 yen" for that particular item. Therefore, if this type of "1-yen sales" were to be applied to all disposed items, the total amount of gross profit on sales would be almost equal to the amount calculated with the ending inventory as the physical inventory; thus, franchisees would be able to blend nearly the entire amount of disposal loss into the cost of goods sold and, as a result, the royalty amount would be small. However, the "negative gross profit on sales" of the item sold at 1 yen is an amount virtually equivalent to the disposal loss, and the store would need to bear the cost of disposal loss.

6   Sharing the Risk of Disposal Loss

If we assume that there is no opening inventory at the moment, the amount of disposal loss would be equal to the difference between the actual order quantity and the actual sales quantity. In other words,

$$
\begin{aligned}
\text{Disposal loss} &= \text{purchase unit price} \\
&\quad \times (\text{actual order quantity} - \text{actual sales quantity}) \\
&= \text{volume variance.}
\end{aligned}
$$

If the purchase cycle is one day in length and unsold goods need to be disposed on the day of arrival, the actual sales quantity would never exceed the actual order quantity. In the case of "actual order quantity < actual sales quantity", the store would be out of stock (see Fig. 2).

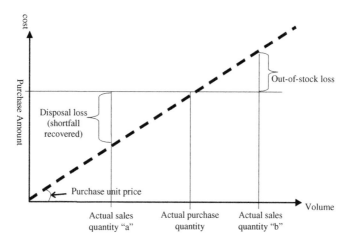

Fig. 2. Disposal loss due to volume variance (Modified from the figure in Monden (2009b), p. 77).

With this type of purchase cycle, convenience foods with very short expiration dates cannot be returned or carried over to the next day as stock. Therefore, the entire purchase cost would be the "fixed cost" of the day. Thus, it is the expense that needs to be spent, regardless of whether or not the goods are sold. The amount unrecovered on this fixed cost would be the unfavorable volume variance, in other words, the disposal loss.

In the same context, there is a custom among the supply chains of the automobile industry in Japan, through which automobile manufacturers share the risk and pay for a part of all equipment (e.g., a stamping dice) when parts manufacturers need to invest in new equipment at the time of developing and producing new cars. In other words, it has been the custom that if the actual sales quantity does not reach the one predicted and set by the assembler, the assembler will provide parts manufacturers a subsidy in consideration of the unrecovered portion of the fixed cost — in this case, of the dice expense. Through this custom, automobile manufacturers provide parts manufacturers with an incentive to invest in new equipment to produce a specific part for new cars. (For further detail, please see Monden and Nagao, 1987–1988; Monden 1991, 1992 and Hoshi, 2007, 2010, inter alia.)

Similarly, in the case of convenience store chains, so long as a franchiser gives its franchisees instructions to minimize "out-of-stock loss" or opportunity loss — even if the final order is to be placed by franchisees — that franchiser should also be held responsible for the occurrence of disposal loss and the like. Therefore, convenience store chains may adopt a system similar to that seen in automobile manufacturing, in which the franchiser would share the risk of disposal loss. We could say that this way of thinking has lead SEJ to a decision where "the franchiser would bear 15% of the disposal loss" (*The Nikkei*, June 24, 2009).

7　Guaranteed Minimum Income of Store Owner

If a store owner is guaranteed a minimum income, it means that the franchiser has shared the risk of making a required minimum profit; this scenario is similar to that in which automobile manufacturers compensate parts manufacturers for the unrecovered cost related to production-equipment expenses.

7.1　*Guaranteed minimums*

Type A (Franchisee candidate who owns land and building)

SEJ guarantees a minimum "owner gross income" (i.e., gross profit on sales minus SEJ's commission) of 19 million yen per year. In other words, if the gross income falls below 19 million yen per year, then the franchiser would compensate the store for the shortfall. This represents a kind of "risk-sharing".[3]

Type C (Franchisee candidate with land and building provided by franchiser)

Bear in mind that, with this type, the franchiser prepares the land and building for the store, and the franchisee need not even pay rent for the property. In this scenario, SEJ offers a guaranteed minimum income of 17 million yen per year.[4]

---

[3]Lawson guarantees 22.2 million yen per year, FamilyMart guarantees 20 million yen per year, and Circle K Sunkus guarantees within the range of "23 million yen $\leq$ (19 million yen + sales volume × 6%) $\leq$ 27 million". Ministop guarantees 21 million yen per year. Circle K Sunkus offers the highest guaranteed minimum of its type.

[4]Lawson guarantees 21 million yen per year; however, if an operational security deposit is required, it then guarantees 22 million yen per year. FamilyMart guarantees 20 million yen per year. Circle K Sunkus guarantees within the range

As stated above, in the case of SEJ, the amount of guaranteed minimum income is dependent on the amount of investment made in the store property; the amount of guaranteed minimum income would be lower if the franchiser had borne the cost of the property. In the cases of other chains, there is a tendency for the guaranteed minimum income to be higher whenever the store owner bears the cost of the property. Clearly, the principles of "low risk, low return" and "high risk, high return" can also be seen here.

8   Terms and Conditions of Other Profit Sharing: Franchise Fee (Deposit Upon Contract), Cost of Utilities, Interior Finishing Work

8.1   *Franchise fee (franchise initial-participating fee; deposit upon contract)*

In terms of franchise fees, unlike other items, only SEJ has different set amounts for Types A and C; they represent "high risk, high return" and "low risk, low return" scenarios, respectively. The following outlines the amount of franchise fee by type.

Franchise fee (deposit upon contract) of Type A (Franchisee candidate who owns land and building): 3,070,5000 yen (tax included) in case of SEJ.[5]

Franchise fee (deposit upon contract) of Type C (Franchisee candidate with land and building provided by franchiser): 2,550,000 yen (tax included) in case of SEJ.[6]

The difference in franchise fees seen here, in the case of SEJ, can be accounted for the differences in "business preparation fees": for Type A, it is 1,050,000 yen, and for Type C, 525,000 yen. With other chains, the franchise fee would be the same for both Type A and Type C.

---

of "20 million yen $\leq$ (14 million yen + sales volume $\times$ 6%) $\leq$ 22 million". Ministop guarantees 21 million yen per year.

[5] Lawson: 3,075,000 yen (tax included)
FamilyMart: 3,075,000 yen (tax included)
Circle K Sunkus: 2,500,000 yen
Ministop: 2,550,000 yen (tax included)

[6] Lawson: 3,075,000 yen (tax included)
FamilyMart: 3,075,000 yen (tax included)
Circle K Sunkus: 2,500,000 yen
Ministop: 2,550,000 yen (tax included)

8.2 *Cost of utilities*

In the case of SEJ, the franchiser pays for 80% of the cost of utilities and the franchisee pays for 20%, regardless of the amount of investment made in the property. For the sake of comparison, in the case of FamilyMart, the franchisee basically bears 100% of the cost of utilities; however, in the case where the franchiser provides the property and bears the cost of exterior and interior finishing work and equipment work, the franchiser pays the portion of the utility costs that exceeds 3.6 million yen per year. In the case of Circle K Sunkus, the franchisee bears the entire utility cost, regardless of the amount of investment made in the property.

8.3 *Differences in the amount to be borne for interior finishing work*

In the cases of SEJ, Lawson, Circle K Sunkus, and Daily Yamazaki, these differences depend on the amount of investment made in the store property; however, a converse relation can be observed compared to the items seen here thus far. In other words, when the franchiser bears the cost of property investment, it also bears the entire cost of interior finishing work. If the store owner bears the cost of property investment, then he or she would bear the cost of interior finishing work. Ultimately, the party who invests in the property is responsible for the cost of maintaining the property.[7]

9 Summary

A summary of the analysis of SEJ is shown in Table 1. What should be noted here is the fact that the royalty rates and guaranteed minimum incomes are dependent upon whether or not an investment was made in the store property.

---

[7]With FamilyMart, there is the case in which the franchisee bears the cost of interior finishing work, even when the franchisee prepares the property (royalty rate: 35%); there is also the case in which the franchiser bears part of the cost (royalty rate: 38%). Also, in the case of Ministop, even with Type C (i.e., property provided by the franchiser), there is the case in which the franchisee bears the cost of interior finishing work (sliding scale royalty system: 36%–58%), and there is another case in which the franchiser bears the cost (sliding scale royalty system: 36%–73%).

Table 1. Correlations among terms and conditions of profit sharing.

	Type A	Type C
Investment in store property	Cost to be brone by franchisee (10–20) million yen)	Cost to be borne by franchiser (Cost incurred by franchisee: 3–5 million yen)
	Franchisee: High risk	Franchisee: Low risk
Royalty rates	Low (43%)	High (56–76%)
	Franchisee: High return	Franchisee: Low return
Sharing the cost of disposal loss	Franchisee: 85%	Franchisee: 15%
Guaranteed minimum income	Big	Small
	Franchisee: High return	Franchisee: Low return
Franchisee fee (Revenue of franchiser)	Big: 3,075,000 yen	Small: 2,550,000 yen
Cost for interior finishing work	Borne by franchise	Borne by franchiser
Cost of utilities	Franchisee: 20%	Franchisee: 80%

In this paper, we mainly analyzed the conditions of profit sharing after becoming a franchisee of a convenience store chain. In Section 3, we refer to differences in profit sharing among various convenience store chains; details are provided in the footnotes.

Differences in the terms of profit sharing among chains (e.g., differences in royalty rates) are something that could help a prospective franchisee determine which chain would be the best to join. Here, multiple convenience store chains form a sort of market in terms of profit sharing, and the principle of market competition plays a role in that market, in terms of obtaining franchisee candidates. This means that the terms of profit sharing — including the royalty rate, the franchiser–franchisee ratio of bearing disposal losses, or the guaranteed minimum income involved — that should be determined upon becoming a franchisee are influenced in a manner similar to that seen with "competing prices" or "market prices". However, competition would not be influenced by the royalty rate alone; there is competition among chains with all kinds of profit-sharing terms intertwined, and so each chain should be screened in terms of a number of different competitive values.

On the other hand, after a franchisee becomes a member of a certain chain, these profit-sharing terms can work as part of an incentive system, in order to achieve cooperation that leads to mutual satisfaction between the franchiser and franchisee, rather than as a component of market competition. This is seen in similar cases, such as when the intra-company transfer price of a divisionalized organization is determined based on the market price, for the sake of a divisional performance evaluation. Here, the idea of mutually satisfactory profit sharing between both parties is valued. Additionally, fairness between the franchiser and franchisee would be considered when changing various profit-sharing terms with current franchisees (e.g., changing terms vis-à-vis royalty rates or the sharing of disposal losses, or adopting a policy that allows for extensions of expiration dates).

Finally, we would like to analyze how and by what kind of mechanism a franchisee's active ordering is motivated, given that a franchiser shares with franchisees disposal-loss risk; we would like to undertake this analysis from the standpoint of statistical decision theory.

To start, we would like to point out the three assumptions made herein. First, let us assume that an outlet of a franchise chain is expecting to make a profit in cooperation with the franchiser, but that the profit will vary according to the uncertainty of the market demands. Let us also assume that this franchisee wants to avoid as much disposal-loss risk as possible (i.e., *risk-avoidant or risk-averter*), and that the franchiser believes that, if it can avoid being out of stock, it is acceptable to have some disposal loss (i.e., the franchiser is not risk-avoidant or *prefers higher risk appetite*).

If such a franchiser thinks that it should share the disposal-loss risk that occurs at the store and hence offers a subsidy for a portion of the franchisee's purchase expenses (in other words, if they would bear a part of the disposal loss), the *expected (average) profit* of the franchisee would be the same, but the *variability (variance)* of the franchisee's profit would become smaller. In such a scenario, the risk of the franchisee would decrease.

The fact that the franchisee's profit would sustain only a small variance means that it is not possible for there to be a broad range of profitability, with running large deficits in worse cases and enjoying large surpluses in better cases. Franchise owners have a large *disutility* for negative earnings (in other words, franchise owners experience considerable *psychological distress* at seeing red figures in their bookkeeping); this is because owners are "risk-avoidant". Since the possibility of having such red figures would be reduced on account of subsidies offered by the franchiser (i.e., by sharing disposal-loss risk), the possibility of disutility increase would be smaller;

therefore, in such a scenario, the *expected (average) utility* of an achievable profit on the part of the franchise owner tends to be a positive figure. For this reason, there are more opportunities to encourage franchisees to place orders actively, without their fear of disposal-loss risk (see Monden and Nagao, 1987–1988; and Monden, 1992).

References

Hoshi, N. (2007). Business model of convenience stores based on a charge base of royalty — Focusing on Seven-Eleven Japan Co., Ltd., in Monden, Y. (ed.), *Japanese Management Accounting Today*, Singapore: World Scientific Pub. Co., 203–216.

Hoshi, N. (2010). Royalties and profit sharing: Focusing on Seven-Eleven Japan Co., Ltd., in Hamada, K. (ed.), *Business Group Management in Japan*, Singapore: World Scientific Pub. Co., 151–161.

Monden, Y. (1991). *Development of Transfer Price and Profit Allocation.* Tokyo: Dobunkan Shuppan (in Japanese).

Monden, Y. (1992). *Cost Management of the New Manufacturing Age: Innovations in the Japanese Automotive Industry*, Cambridge, MA: Productivity Press.

Monden, Y. (2009a). M&A and its incentive system for the inter-firm organization, in Kurokawa, Y. (ed.), *M&A for Value Creation in Japan*, Singapore: World Scientific Pub. Co., 67–89.

Monden, Y. (2009b). *Profit Allocation Price for the Inter-Firm Cooperation*, Tokyo: Zeimukeirikyokai (in Japanese).

Monden, Y. (2010). Acquisition price as an incentive price of M&A, in Hamada, K. (ed.), *Business Group Management in Japan*, Singapore: World Scientific Pub. Co., 73–91.

Monden, Y. (2012). From Adam Smith's division of labor to the network organization: From the market price mechanism to the incentive price mechanism, In Monden, Y. (ed.), *Management of an Inter-Firm Network*, Singapore: World Scientific Pub. Co., 3–30.

Monden, Y. and T. Nagao (1987–1988). Full cost-based transfer pricing in the Japanese auto industry: Risk-sharing and risk-spreading behavior, *Journal of Business Administration*, 17(1–2), 117–136.

Mouritsen, J. and S. Thrane (2006). Accounting, network complementarities and the development of inter-organizational relations, *Accounting, Organizations and Society*, 31, 241–275.

Sakakibara, K. (ed.) (2010). *Gekkan Conveni.* 11, 14 (in Japanese).

Takeuchi, M. (2001). *A Book for Convenience Stores Owners*. Tokyo: Shogyokai (in Japanese).

The Nikkei. (2009). Seven-Eleven compensates for the disposal loss of rice boll by 15%. June 24, 9.

Supplementary Reference Resources

Circle K Sunkus website. Available at http://www.circleksunkus.jp/member/owner/contract. Aceessed April 11, 2011.

Daily Yamazaki website. Available at http://www.daily-yamazaki.co.jp/jn/type.html. Accessed May 2, 2011.

FamilyMart website. Available at http://fc.family.co.jp/2fc/; http://fc.family.co.jp/standalone/contract/owner/; http://fc.family.co.jp/standalone/contract/fm. Accessed April 11, 2011.

Lawson website. Available at: http://www.lawson.co.jp/company/fc/owner/affiliate. Accessed April 11, 2011.

MINISTOP website. Available at http://www.ministop.co.jp/franchise. Accessed April 11, 2011.

Seven-Eleven Japan website, Available at http://www.sej.co.jp/owner/keiyaku. Accessed April 11, 2011.

2

Profit Management in the Hotel Industry

Akimichi Aoki
Senshu University

1   Introduction

In many Japanese hotels, the technique called "revenue management" (also called yield management) has been widely introduced and used for price and capacity control. Nevertheless, RevPAR, which is mostly known as an outcome measure for revenue management, is not widely used in Japanese hotels because of revenue control practices initiated by "real" travel agent companies, especially in hotels located in rural areas.

This article examines the reason why many Japanese lodging businesses do not emphasize RevPAR and explains the effect of real travel agents on sales revenue control implemented in Japanese hotels. It will also show that pseudo-revenue management is implemented in parallel with primary revenue management.

2   Overview of Revenue Management

2.1   *Background and definition of revenue management*

Services are intangible goods (Regan, 1963; Fitzsimmons and Fitzsimmons, 1994) and perish at the same time as production. Since they perish when produced, services cannot be stored like physical goods. Also, maximum sales amounts are restricted by the initial capacity. As most capacity costs are fixed costs, in the short run, revenue maximization has stronger effects on the increase of profit than cost reduction in capacity-restricted service industries such as hotels, airline companies, movie theaters, broadcasting companies, and so on.

To increase sales revenue in the short run, many hotels use a technique called revenue management. Revenue management is the practice of obtaining the highest possible revenue in the selling of a service firm's capacity (Ng, 2008). In relation to hotels, revenue management is a revenue maximization tool, which aims to increase net yield through the predicated allocation of available bedroom capacity to predetermined market segments at optimal price (Donaghy and McMahon, 1995). Revenue management does not only try to enhance the turnover ratio (or capacity usage ratio) of the site but also is a technique that can increase the short-term sales revenue.

2.2 *Price discrimination and sales increase*

Sales revenue will increase if price control is implemented promptly. This section explains the reason using a simple example (see Fig. 1). Hotel A is a mid-sized hotel that has 500 rooms. For simplicity, this example has the assumption that its 500 rooms are all of the same type. The diagonal line from top left to bottom right in the figure is the demand curve, which shows how many rooms would be sold at a given price. For example, Hotel A

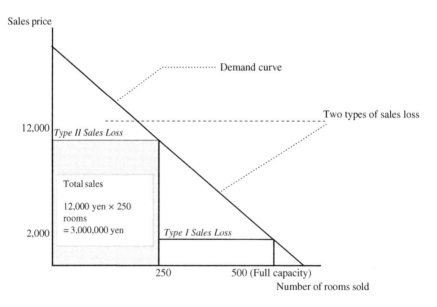

Fig. 1.   Revenue maximization with rack rate.

can sell 500 rooms (full capacity) if the sales price is set at 2,000 yen, and sales will be zero if the sales price is set at 22,000 yen. To maximize sale revenue, Hotel A should set its price at 12,000 yen and sales revenue would be 3,000,000 yen. But, if Hotel A sets its rack rate and set price at one point, Hotel A could lose two types of sales revenue as shown below:

Type I Sales Loss: Sales loss from customers who had intended to buy the service goods but did not do so as the goods are very expensive.

Type II Sales Loss: Sale loss from customers who had intended to buy the service goods at a higher rate but bought the goods at the rack rate.

To increase sales revenue, Hotel A should discriminate prices while setting fences around price ranges to avoid the transshipment of customers from a higher price range to a lower price range (see Fig. 2). The role of these fences is the switching costs of customers. In this example, Hotel A sets three types of price range and would receive 4,500,000 yen (17,000 yen × 125 persons + 12,000 yen × 125 persons + 7,000 yen × 125 persons) if fences function correctly. Many hotels discriminate price ranges by setting various accommodation plans and changing prices depending on their booking situation to maximize sales revenue.

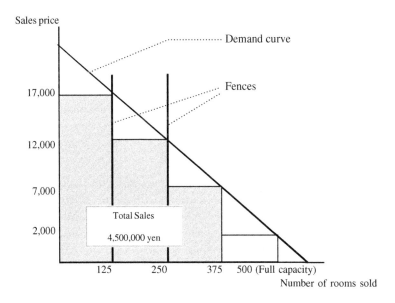

Fig. 2.   Revenue maximization with price discrimination.

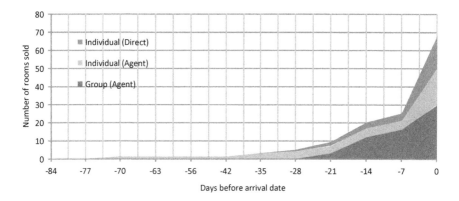

Fig. 3.   Example of booking curve.

2.3 *Booking curve*

Booking curve refers to the pattern at which reservations for the hotel were requested and accepted (Tranter *et al.*, 2009). Figure 3 shows the typical example of a booking curve. The booking curve shows when each customer segment tends to reserve rooms. This graph shows the situation of booking for a given day by three customer segments and becomes the basic data for demand forecasting, which is the act of estimating and predicting consumers' future demand. By comparing demand estimation calculated using past data and actual status of reservation, the manager of the hotel would decide whether a new accommodation plan should be made or not, whether the existing plan should increase or decrease price, and whether more capacity (rooms) should be allocated to the popular plan or not.

2.4 *RevPAR as an outcome measure*

The outcome measure of revenue management is yield, which means revenue per available time-based inventory (James and Chekitan, 1999). In lodging industries, yield is calculated as RevPAR, which is determined by dividing room revenue received for a period by the number of rooms available in the hotel for that period, and is the product of multiplying the ADR (Average Daily Rate) and room occupancy rate (see Equation (1)).

$$\text{RevPAR} = \frac{\text{Room revenue}}{\text{Number of rooms sold}} \times \frac{\text{Number of rooms sold}}{\text{Number of rooms available}} \qquad (1)$$

RevPAR is a financial as well as an outcome measure. Banker *et al.* (2005) stated that the RevPAR is positively related to the index of customer satisfaction, which is thought to be the best measure to judge the outcome of revenue management, as ADR and room occupancy rate usually work as a trade-off. To enhance ADR, the manager usually needs to decrease the room occupancy rate. Also, to increase the room occupancy rate, the manager needs to lower the price, which leads to a decrease in ADR. To increase RevPAR, the manager has to pursue a balanced enhancement of ADR and occupancy simultaneously.

3   Revenue Management in Japanese Hotels

3.1   *KPI used in Japanese hotels*

As indicated in the prior section, though the key performance indicator (KPI) for measuring results of revenue management practice is RevPAR, Japanese hotels actually use various other measures as a performance indicator as well. For example, as depicted in Table 1, Shimizu and Otani (2010) found that the most used KPI in Japanese hotels is the room occupancy ratio (98.6%). RevPAR is used only in 67.1% of Japanese hotels (see Table 1). In addition, Aoki and Uetake (2009) implemented a questionnaire survey to 37 Japanese resort hotels in Japan and found that ADR is mostly used in peak travel season while room occupancy rate is mostly used in the off season.

3.2   *The characteristics of real agents and net agents*

In Japan, many customers reserve rooms directly or through travel agents. Travel agents can be categorized as real agents and net agents. Real agents

Table 1.   KPI used in lodging division in Japanese hotels.

Performance indicator	Frequency ($N = 70$) multiple answers allowed	Ratio (%)
ADR (Average Daily Ratio)	56	80.0
Room occupancy ratio	69	98.6
RevPAR	47	67.1
Cost to Sales Ratio	23	32.9

Table 2. Differences between two types of travel agents in Japan.

Type of agents	Fee paid to agents	Lead time	Change of price	Change of the number of rooms
Real agents	high	long	impossible	impossible
Net agents	low	short	possible	possible

are travel agent companies that have many locations in convenient places such as JTB Corp and Kinki Nippon Tourist (KNT). Net agents are travel agents that have virtual shops and sell goods via the Internet such as Rakuten Travel and Jaran.net. As for the revenue control of hotels, each type of agent has different characteristics, as depicted in Table 2.

Traditionally, many Japanese hotels and real agents worked together closely. Especially, hotels located in remote areas, rural areas, and small towns allot a specific number of their rooms preliminarily to be sold on a commitment basis. Sales prices through real agents are decided through preliminary negotiation and contract. They block these rooms throughout the year, so the manager of the hotel cannot change the sales price and allocate a number of rooms for the agent after the annual contract is made. It might be natural for the manager to think of negotiation and contract with real agents as the key for revenue control. Also, the number of controllable rooms is limited, and the effects of revenue management, which are needed to implement flexible prices and capacity control, are definite. Any unsold rooms are returned to the hotel at a predefined date (usually 7–14 days before check-in date).

During the peak season, as rooms are usually sold out, many managers of Japanese hotels only have to worry about overbooking, and the total sales revenue will be decided by the number of rooms that are reserved via the primary branded agent, whose prices are relatively high. In the off-season, the hotel manager usually sells predicted unsold rooms at a lower price before return date from the real agent. Though the commission fee paid to real agents is relatively high, Japanese hotels are able to reduce sales staff by setting aside sales activities.

As for sales through net agents, the manager of the hotel can change the price and number of rooms allocated to a given plan at any time, depending on the reservation status. The manager pays commission fees to net agents when they sell rooms via the net agent's portal site. Though the commission fee is relatively low, the sales price tends to be low too. So the manager has to decide the price of each plan and the number of rooms that should be allocated to each plan, in addition to deciding when to stop selling each plan independently. In an environment where agents do business via the Internet, the condition for implementing revenue management is put in place.

3.3 *Pseudo-revenue management in Japanese lodging industries*

In a situation where most rooms are allotted to real agents, it is difficult to change the sales price depending on the status of reservation, as sales activities are initiated by real agents. Also as depicted in Table 3, targeted customer segments, price range, and lead time are different in various brands. Under such circumstances, hotels control price and allocation of their capacity by negotiating with various types of agents depending on the status of reservation.

Sales of rooms which start at primary and secondary brands have a long lead time. According to the situation of reservation, the hotel manager decides whether he/she should sell their rooms to tertiary branded agents or not for the given period, as well as how many rooms should be allotted to them. Before arriving at the two- or three-week point, the manager must decide whether he/she should sell the remaining rooms to local agents that are devoted to closed segments and do not have considerable effects on price range of the hotel. Similarly, when the hotel has customer membership organization, which is another closed segment, he/she might allot rooms to the organization to enhance customer loyalty according to the status.

Table 3.   Various brands and lead time of commercial travel goods.

Category	Contents	Lead time	Price range
Primary brand	Travel tour projected by major travel company or agent	6 months–12 months	high
Secondary brand	Travel tour projected by second-tier travel company or agent	6 months–12 months	
Tertiary brand	Travel tour directed to low-end consumers	1 month–6 months	
Local brand	Travel tour directed only to local consumers	1 week–3 weeks	low

As these revenue control practices have similarity with primary revenue management, this article refers to these practices as pseudo-revenue management. As with primary revenue management, the manager sells rooms at the rack rate in the early stage and in a lower price range as the arrival date approaches. In this type of revenue management, the transition of customers from high-price tours to low-price tours tends not to occur, as each of the tours are projected by different travel companies and transition would cause a cancellation fee according to contract clause. In pseudo-revenue management, the cancellation fee becomes the switching cost and fills the role of fences around price range.

4 Conclusion

This article examined the differences between primary revenue management and pseudo-revenue management practice implemented in Japanese lodging businesses initiated by real travel agents. Traditionally, many Japanese hotels relied on real travel agents for their sales activities, and their revenue control is implemented through the decision of when and how many rooms should be allotted to each agent. Each agent has different price range, customer segments, and lead time. Also, as per consumer contract with each company, the cancellation fee becomes the switching cost for customers. As a consequence, Japanese hotels are able to keep revenue control in place by entering a contract with proper agents, allocating the remaining rooms in prompt time, and do not need to watch RevPAR. This article referred to this practice as pseudo-revenue management.

Recently, the amount of reservations sold via net agents is increasing. Hotel managers are able to implement primary revenue management practice by selling their rooms via net agents. Though it is difficult to sell rooms at lower price at the last minute without fences, an early bird discount system is usually adopted as a pricing system. As a result, two types of pricing systems exist in parallel. In the future, this will give rise to a problem of how to control the two types of price control systems simultaneously.

References

Aoki, A. and T. Uetake (2009). Analysis of revenue management system in resort hotels: Mail survey (in Japanese), *Bulletin of the Institute of Business Administration*, No. 179, 1–32.

Banker, R. D., G. Potter and D. Srinivasan (2005). Association of nonfinancial measures with the financial performance of a lodging chain, *Cornell Hotel and Restaurant Administration Quarterly,* November, 394–412.

Donaghy, K. and U. McMahon (1995). Yield management — a marketing perspective, *International Journal of Vacation Marketing,* 2(1), 55–62.

Fitzsimmons, J. A. and M. J. Fitzsimmons (1994). *Service Management — Operations, Strategy, Information Technology,* New York: McGraw-Hill.

James, B. R. and D. S. Chekitan (1999). Look beyond RevPAR, *Cornell Hotel & Restaurant Administration Quarterly,* 40(2), 23–31.

Ng, I. C. L. (2008). *The Pricing and Revenue Management of Services — A Strategic Approach,* New York: Routledge.

Regan, W. J. (1963). The service revolution, *The Journal of Marketing,* 27(3), 57–62.

Shimizu, T. and H. Otani (2010). The practice of management accounting for the lodging industry in Japan, *Waseda Syogaku* (in Japanese) 424, 1–30.

Tranter, K. A., T. Stuart-Hill and J. Parker (2009). *An Introduction to Revenue Management for the Hospitality Industries — Principles and Practices for the Real World,* Pearson Education.

3

Kaizen Activities and Performance Management in the Sales Finance Business

Noriyuki Imai
Meijo University

1 Introduction

The publication of "Innovation America" (a.k.a. the Palmisano Report) in December 2004 by the U.S. Council on Competitiveness, a non-profit organization, gave rise to the academic field of "service science". Against the backdrop of the global economic shift into services, this field was concerned with creating an engine for economic growth through innovation and enhanced productivity in the service sector.

One example of a Japanese service company that has been able to maintain a high level of competitiveness and thrive on the global stage is the sales finance unit of Toyota Motor Corp. This chapter provides insight into the *kaizen* (improvement) activities and performance management that form the cornerstone of the competitiveness of Toyota's sales finance unit.

2 Auto Sales and Sales Finance at Toyota

Toyota — the largest automotive maker in Japan and one of the foremost in the world — has been able to overcome numerous headwinds since its establishment in 1937, such as the management crisis in 1950, the oil shock, tighter environmental regulations, trade frictions, a strong yen, the collapse of the bubble economy, and the fallout of the bankruptcy of Lehman Brothers. Presently, Toyota is one of the world's pre-eminent global companies, producing over 7.5 million cars in over 27 countries/regions and selling them in over 170 countries/regions worldwide. In tandem with its automotive business, Toyota has also been active in the sales finance business.

When Toyota was established in 1937, the Japanese automotive market was dominated by American manufacturers, Ford and General Motors (GM). Both Ford and GM built assembly plants in Japan in 1924 and 1926, respectively. In addition, both companies expanded their operations in Japan by establishing finance companies — GM in 1927 and Ford in 1928 — that enabled consumers to purchase cars by paying in monthly instalments. Toyota, who was a late entrant into the market, began competing with Ford and GM in 1937, with the creation of its own monthly installment–based sales finance function.

The 1950s and 1960s were the periods of popularization of automobiles in Japan. With the implementation of the Installment Sales Act in 1961, those who sold cars under installment plans were able to retain the titles on such, and were now required by law to clarify the terms of the installment sale to their customers and provide them with a contract copy, among other obligations. With the debut of the Publica in 1961, Toyota also developed and introduced the "Publica Note" as a way for paying installments by cheque. This served as a promissory note to market the Publica to consumers who did not have a checking account at a bank and was the impetus for the cheque collateral system becoming the standard method of collecting on debts.

The Publica Note was renamed to the "Toyota Note" in 1966 and was adopted across the company's entire line of vehicles. Toyota widened the scope of their sales finance business with the debut of the Corolla in 1966, introducing products and services aimed at increasing sales to individuals (particularly salaried workers), such as the bonus-linked payment plan, the long-term payment plan and group credit life insurance supplements.

The enormous amount of cheque processing that was required was streamlined when the bank transfer option was added to the Toyota Note in 1976. The system was again renamed to "Toyota Credit". The company continued to broaden its line-up of auto sales finance products and services, and the sales finance business has continued to develop hand-in-hand with the automotive business.

3 The Sales Finance Business Model

There are generally two types of business models in sales finance: the core business synergy model and the independent model.

In the core business synergy model, the company introduces the various management resources and expertise of the core business unit into the sales finance unit to bolster the latter's management foundation, while the latter actively supports the sales promotion of the former by offering financial services to the core unit's customers.

This model is based on David Aaker's concept of diversification. Igor Ansoff has pointed out that when penetration is difficult in existing markets with existing products, firms have three options for diversifying strategy: (1) developing new products for existing markets, (2) breaking into new markets with existing products, and (3) developing new products for new markets, or "diversification in the narrow sense" (Ansoff, 1957). In addition to Ansoff's two pillars of products and markets, Aaker also added "business systems" as the third pillar of diversification, which includes elements such as procurement, production, distribution, technology, and marketing (Aaker, 1984). That is, the core business synergy model, in which the core and sales finance businesses share customers and supplement each other's marketing, management and know-how, is a business model that facilitates diversification within a set boundary of business risk.

A representative example of this model is the sales finance business of GM and Ford during the 1980s and 1990s. While the sales finance units of both companies at the time received support from the automotive units in acquiring capital, the finance units in turn contributed greatly to promoting auto sales by offering a variety of financial services — such as auto leasing, auto insurance, rental cars, home loans and credit cards — to auto customers.

In the independent model, on the other hand, the company does not actively pursue synergies between the core business unit and the sales finance unit, but rather the finance unit is independent of the core unit and develops its own business independently. This model is based on Alfred Rappaport's concept of shareholder value management. Rappaport argued that managers must build shareholder value by realizing earnings that exceed the expected return of investors (shareholders) and ensuring a steady flow of residual income (Rappaport, 1986). In this model, the sales finance unit is free from all the various restraints that accompany a collaborative relationship with the core unit in business management. The finance unit contributes to the core business unit — one of its shareholders — by singularly pursing maximum revenue as a finance business.

A representative example of this model is GE's sales finance business during the period from the late 1980s to 1990s. Jack Welch, the CEO of GE during that period, implemented a dynamic business model in the company's sales finance unit, which combined aggressive M&A with bold downsizing of the business (Welch and Byrne, 2001). As a rule, Welch limited M&A targets to firms that were the leading or number two companies in their field and set a clear hurdle rate of 15%–20% expected return to investment. By relentlessly demanding this performance from the managers of target companies, the finance unit contributed greatly to GE's consolidated earnings.

As Toyota entered the 1980s, in tandem with the full-fledged globalization of the automotive business, the sales finance business also expanded its activities abroad. At this time, the finance unit adopted the core business synergy model. The reason for this was twofold. First, the broad customer base of Toyota's core automotive business also included significant potential customers for the sales finance business. Second, by incorporating the management expertise of Toyota's automotive unit cultivated over many years since its creation — specifically the ideas and techniques of one of Toyota's core competencies, *"kaizen"* — into the sales finance unit, the company aimed to fundamentally bolster the management base of the latter.

4 Toyota's Sales Finance Business Activities

The surge in the overseas automobile production growth necessitated a much stronger sales force outside Japan, and Toyota expanded the operations of its sales finance business globally as part of its strategy. It established Toyota Motor Credit Corporation (TMCC) in the U.S. in 1982 as an auto sales finance company, and similarly established Toyota Finance Australia Ltd. (TFA) in Australia. Furthermore, in 1988, the sales finance business in Japan broke off from the auto (core) business to form Toyota Finance Corporation (TFC). Toyota subsequently went on to establish other auto sales finance companies worldwide, with operations in 10 countries/regions by 1997 and 33 countries/regions till date.

Meanwhile, Japan fell into a long-term economic slump in the 1990s following the collapse of the bubble economy. The structure of the Japanese auto market experienced changes such as units sold stabilizing at a low level, demand shifting toward the smaller car segment, and consumers holding onto their cars for a longer period of time. In addition, the external environment surrounding Toyota's sales finance business was undergoing a significant transformation, with restructuring and escalating competition between banks, non-banks and other financial institutions in the Japanese financial sector in addition to tougher and more diverse customer demands in financial services.

In response to this changing environment, Toyota established Toyota Financial Services Corp. (TFS) in 2000 to unify the administration of its global sales finance business strategy and operations, and to act as a management company for developing and launching new financial products to meet new customer demands. Presently, TFS offers financial services such as auto leasing and loans to Toyota customers in 33 countries and regions worldwide. Furthermore, in Japan, the company contributes to auto sales by providing a wide variety of financial services to individual customers in addition to auto loans, such as credit cards, securities, and asset management (including investment trusts and pensions).

Currently, the sales finance business of TFS manages a total of approximately 13 trillion yen in assets around the world and employs approximately 8,000 people. TFS is a global financial institution representing Japan, being the largest sales finance company in the country and one of the pre-eminent financial institutions in the world.

5   *Kaizen* Activities in Toyota's Sales Finance Business

As stated earlier, the business model of Toyota's sales finance unit is the "core business synergy model." In this model, the company introduces the various management resources and expertise of the core business unit, which is the automotive unit, into the sales finance unit to bolster the latter's management foundation. At the same time, the latter actively supports the sales promotion of the core unit by offering financial services to its customers.

As mentioned previously, one of the main elements introduced into the sales finance unit from the automotive unit is the management expertise cultivated over many years at Toyota's automotive production plants — specifically the views on and techniques of one of Toyota's core competencies, "*kaizen*". The *kaizen* views and techniques at Toyota and examples of the framework for promoting *kaizen* activities in Toyota's sales finance business are outlined below.

5.1   *The Toyota way* — Kaizen *thinking*

Kaizen thinking has become formally known as the "Toyota Way". As previously stated, automobile production at Toyota grew dramatically outside Japan from the mid-1980s, and the company has created an enterprise that is presently spread across 27 countries and regions around the world and produces over 7.5 million cars. Over the course of this process, the management has faced the critical issue of introducing the *kaizen* thinking — based on the Toyota Production System (TPS) — to the workers in its production hubs based outside Japan.

Toyota introduced the Toyota Way in 2001 to solve this problem. This is a scheme (psychological framework) in which the company has cultivated unspoken knowledge developed over years on production factory floors in Japan — *kaizen* thinking. This formal knowledge has been called the DNA of Toyota.

The framework of the Toyota Way is as follows:

1. Continuous Improvement

    (a) Challenge: We form a long-term vision, meeting challenges with courage and creativity to realize our dreams.
    (b) *Kaizen*: We improve our business operations continuously, always driving for innovation and evolution.
    (c) *Genchi Genbutsu*: We practice *genchi genbutsu*... go to the source to find the facts to make correct decisions, build consensus, and achieve goals at our best speed.

2. Respect for People

    (a) Respect: We respect others, make every effort to understand each other, take responsibility, and do our best to build mutual trust.
    (b) Teamwork: We stimulate personal and professional growth, share the opportunities of development, and maximize individual and team performance.

At Toyota, stability of life, self-fulfilment, and personal growth of employees and growth of the business are two sides of the same coin. The company believes that mutual trust between employees and management, long-term stability, and communication form the mental foundation necessary for this growth.

Based on this foundation, the Toyota Way is composed of the two pillars of "continuous improvement" and "respect for people", and is further broken down into the five keywords of "challenge", "*kaizen*", "*genchi genbutsu*", "respect", and "teamwork".

"Continuous improvement" means never being satisfied with things as they are and continuously thinking hard for ways to increase added value. "Respect for people" means respecting all stakeholders and linking employees' personal growth to the performance of the company.

There are three key ideas inherent in the Toyota Way:

First is the idea of going to the source to find the facts. What is not explicitly stated here is that employees are admonished not to make decisions based only on data such as accounting numbers and that the company staunchly insists that employees dig deep to find the true root of problems when they occur.

Second is the idea of mutual understanding and mutual responsibility. This idea emphasizes mutual relationships within a process, which can be characterized as relentlessly working and contemplating together.

Third is the idea of maximizing team performance, which also means functional integration. *Kaizen* is the driver of the evolution of management organization structure through these united functions.

5.2 *Problem solving methodology — The techniques of* Kaizen

The techniques of Toyota's *kaizen* are based on methods that are widely known as problem-solving methods. Recently, this has been referred to within Toyota as "Toyota Business Practice".

These problem-solving techniques are the result of statistical quality control (SQC) and total quality control (TQC). These ideas belong to W. Edwards Deming, the widely recognized leading thinker in the field of quality.

W. Edwards Deming is acknowledged as one of the people who were most influential in transforming the Japanese economy following WWII. At that time, the U.S. was the leading economic powerhouse and its products were the subject of envy worldwide. Japan, on the other hand, was aware that its own products paled in comparison to those of the U.S., but they did not have the economic capacity to simply dispose the materials of those products that failed inspection after they were completed. Deming was invited to come to Japan as a statistician, and his methods were widely disseminated across all industries in Japan. This quality control movement was one of the key factors that enabled Japan's manufacturing industry to become internationally competitive.

Deming's ideas of SQC and TQC focused on the importance of randomness in the sense of things not going according to plan. He argued that (1) randomness exists in all systems, (2) the cause of most of this randomness was fixed within designs, processes, and systems and (3) it was the management's responsibility to prevent the recurrence of this randomness.

In his later years, Deming outlined the following 14 principles of management (Deming, 1982):

1. Create constancy of purpose toward improvement of product and service.
2. Adopt the new philosophy.
3. Cease dependence on inspection to achieve quality.
4. End the practice of awarding business on the basis of price tag.
5. Improve constantly and forever the system of production and service.
6. Institute training on the job.
7. Institute leadership.
8. Drive out fear.
9. Break down barriers between departments.
10. Eliminate slogans, exhortations, and targets for the workforce.
11. Eliminate work standards (quotas) on the factory floor, management by objective, management by numbers, and numerical goals.
12. Remove barriers that rob the hourly paid worker and people in management and engineering of their right to pride in workmanship.
13. Institute a vigorous program of education and self-improvement.
14. Put everybody in the company to work to accomplish the transformation.

Toyota's method of problem-solving is based on Deming's methods of SQC and TQC. In this method, whenever randomness causes the current situation to deviate from the norm (i.e., how things should be), the entire company cooperates to immediately enact the cycle of (1) identifying the problem, (2) analyzing the current situation, (3) setting objectives, (4) investigating the causes, (5) developing an action plan, (6) implementing the plan (7) verifying the outcome, and (8) adopting other measures. This cycle is commonly known as the plan–do–check–act (PDCA) cycle, or the Deming cycle.

Toyota utilizes this problem-solving method as a *kaizen* technique. Toyota's *kaizen* technique, however, has two notable characteristics. The first is digging deep to pin down the true source of the problem by asking the "Five Whys" and taking action to completely prevent the problem from reoccurring. The second is providing all employees with an opportunity to receive training on problem-solving methodologies, and hence continuously maintain a state throughout the entire management framework in which employees are empowered to independently make improvements at any time.

5.3 *Framework for the promotion of* kaizen *activities in the sales finance business*

Building on the "Toyota Way" as *kaizen* thinking and on the problem-solving method as a *kaizen* technique, TFS systemizes the methods for promoting *kaizen* activities in Toyota's sales finance business. This program is called "global best practice" (GBP).

GBP consists of three elements: (1) education and training, (2) practicing *kaizen*, and (3) contests.

(1) Education and training

In addition to the "Toyota Way" and problem-solving methodologies, education and training encompasses aspects such as the Toyota production system (TPS) and the "seven wastes" — areas to focus on for *kaizen*. Educational contents that cover these are perpetually prepared in both English and Japanese. As a general rule, the approximately 8,000 employees in 33 countries and regions worldwide all receive training on these materials through the intranet-based e-learning program.

(2) Practicing *kaizen*

Kaizen is practised not as a task that is separate from everyday duties; rather, it is practised continuously throughout the whole workplace in unison with these duties. This everyday aspect of *kaizen* is a characteristic unique to *kaizen* at Toyota and is also present in GBP.

(3) Contests

A yearly *kaizen* contest is held in which sales finance companies in all 33 countries and regions participate. The contest is held at the sales finance company, regional, and global levels, and the winning team at the global level receives an award from the head of TFS. This contest is held on a regular basis and contributes greatly to motivating their employees from the above-mentioned company branches to engage in *kaizen* activities.

5.4 *Examples of* kaizen *in the sales finance business*

The following are some model examples of *kaizen* in GBP.

(1) *Kaizen* in the credit card issuing process

TFC (the sales finance business in Japan) issues credit cards to Toyota's auto customers and provides a variety of different services that contribute to auto sales. For example, if customers use their cards for everyday shopping, they earn points equal to 1% of the total amount spent. Customers can accumulate these points and use them to avail of discounts toward their next car purchase at an advantageous conversion rate. Thus, in this framework, by encouraging customers who purchased a car from Toyota to use the credit cards issued to them for everyday shopping, we find that they return to Toyota when the time comes to replace their cars. TFC has issued approximately eight million cards to date, and approximately 200 employees are responsible for making new issues and renewals. The unique awareness that work results are the same, no matter who does it, is an idea that has been firmly ingrained amongst employees who are in charge of such so-called back-office jobs. Therefore, TFC subsequently executed a targeted implementation of *kaizen* in the credit-card–issuing process in keeping with the GBP program. In accordance with the problem-solving methodology cycle, *kaizen* was performed with the participation of all 200 or so employees. Since this is a particularly large-scale work process, TFC adopted the techniques of "material and information flowcharting" and "stack surveying" unique to the company to analyze the current situation. Material and information flowcharting is a process-mapping technique in which the workflow and relationship between different tasks are made visible by sequentially attaching the materials and ledgers used in these tasks to a long sheet of roll-craft paper. All employees then identify problem areas within the work process as a whole. Stack surveying is a work-time analysis technique in which all employees examine how they spend their time throughout the day in one-minute increments in order to make waste more visible. As a result, TPS embarked on a whole-scale redesign as well as reconstruction of its work processes through actions such as *jidoka* (autonomation), implementing the single flow line, and thoroughly eliminating the "seven wastes". By doing this, TPS was able to realize immense *kaizen* achievements, such as cutting the lead time to card issuance by 40%, improving overall work efficiency by 8%, and greatly enhancing customer satisfaction through aspects such as revising card applications from the perspective of their customers. Furthermore, the company made breakthrough enhancements in the awareness of their 200 or so employees toward *kaizen*.

(2) Curtailing credit screening time

After a customer applies to purchase a vehicle at a Toyota dealership, TFS' sales finance companies must complete a credit screening within a certain timeframe (say, 30 minutes) and report the results to the dealership before offering an auto lease or loan. There has been a trend, however, of losing business opportunities because several times screening results do not return within this timeframe. Here, again, *kaizen* activities made in accordance with GBP have resulted in more precise projections of screening workloads through better collaboration with dealerships, reviewing of screeners' allocation based on hour and day of the week and establishment of a system for employees to give and receive support from each other through education and training. Efforts such as these have dramatically raised the ratio of credit screening results that return on time in many regions.

These are only a few typical examples of *kaizen* in GBP; many other instances of effective *kaizen* are continuously practised in tandem with everyday activities at TFS' sales finance companies, who share this know-how through contests and other activities. Maintaining this type of system of sharing know-how through horizontal collaboration is the reason why TFS' method of promoting *kaizen* activities is known as GBP.

6   Performance Management in Toyota's Sales Finance Business

This chapter has, thus far, described the development, business model, and *kaizen* activities of Toyota's sales finance business. Building on this, the chapter concludes by examining the relationship between performance management and *kaizen* activities in the sales finance business. The main method of performance management at Toyota's sales finance business is period earnings management that utilizes the earnings plan system. Earnings at the business are generally calculated as follows:

$$\text{Sales finance business earnings}$$
$$= \text{loan profit margin} - \text{credit costs} - \text{SG\&A}. \qquad (1)$$

When conducting period earnings management, TFS, the management company, first sets a period earnings target for each sales finance company based on Equation (1). It then communicates this target to each company through the earnings plan system and oversees these companies throughout the accounting year to ensure that they meet these targets.

To meet the period earnings target established by TFS in the beginning of the period, the operations, finance, credit management, administration, and other divisions at each sales finance company each take on a role to fulfil this mission by working to increase loans, optimize interest rates, curb capital acquisition costs, shrink bad loan and leasing expenses, and contain SG&A expenses throughout the accounting year.

Similar to the period earnings control observed in many other companies, performance management in Toyota's sales finance business is thus "vertical-style management", which encompasses the elements of control, meeting goals and division by period, company, and division.

Conversely, as previously stated, *kaizen* activities in Toyota's sales finance business are an instance of "horizontal-style management", which encompasses horizontal collaboration, autonomy, and emergence. Moreover, the benefits of *kaizen* activities are limited to aspects that are only measurable in accounting terms. For example, while reduced expenses through the elimination of waste can be observed by accounting, increased customer satisfaction, and the effective utilization (optimal placement) of employees that accompanies improvements in work efficiency cannot be measured directly.

All these benefits, however, are extremely important effects that testify to the significance of *kaizen* itself. In other words, *kaizen* is not something that is practised with accounting results in mind; what is achieved through practicing *kaizen* has both accounting and non-accounting upshots. Thus, operations in Toyota's sales finance business are divided into "vertical-style management" (performance management and period earnings management) and "horizontal-style management" (*kaizen* activities). In other words, this dichotomized perspective encompasses phase differences such as vertical division and horizontal collaboration perspectives, top-down and bottom-up perspectives, headquarters and on-site (i.e., individual sales finance company) perspectives, accounting and non-accounting perspectives, control and autonomy perspectives, and goal-achieving and emergence perspectives. Furthermore, by incorporating the accounting-measurable outcomes of kaizen into period earnings control through the earnings plan system, the company is able to meld the two characteristically different frameworks of vertical- and horizontal-style management into one system of business administration. Here, one can observe the unique qualities of the "Dual-mode Management Accounting Model" that encompasses the relationship between performance management and *kaizen* activities in Toyota's sales finance business (Imai, 2010).

7   Conclusion

Christopher Lovelock and Jochen Wirtz, two pioneers in the field of service marketing, pointed out that the essence of service management is how well a company can unify the three basic functions of operation management, marketing management, and human resource management to the customer's benefit (Lovelock and Wirtz, 2006).

Similarly, James Heskett, W. Earl Sasser, and Leonard Schlesinger have introduced the concept of the service profit chain (SPC) (Heskett, Sasser, and Schlesinger, 1997). They explain that customer loyalty and the service value that comprises the source of customer satisfaction is dependent on the system for providing services. This system in turn is based on human resources — that is, the productivity, skills, satisfaction, and loyalty of the employees that provide such services.

The *kaizen* activities and performance management of Toyota's sales finance business outlined in this chapter incorporate the essence of these concepts of service management and SPC. It is a highly unique management administration system that is unlike any other in the world, and at the same time, it possesses a universal quality that makes it usable and effective on a global level.

References

Aaker, D. A. (1984). *Strategic Market Management*, Hobokeu, NJ: John Wiley and Sons.

Ansoff, H. I. (1957). Strategies for diversification, *Harvard Business Review*, 35(5), 113–124.

Deming, W. E. (1982). *Out of the Crisis*, Cambridge, MA: Massachusetts Institute of Technology Press.

Heskett, J. L., W. E. Sasser and L. A. Schlesinger (1997). *The Service Profit Chain*, New York: Free Press.

Imai, N. (2010). The proposal of dual-mode management accounting model: Aiming at the dissolution of "accounting lag," *The Meijo Review*, 10(4), 61–87 (in Japanese).

Lovelock, C. H. and J. Wirtz (2006), *Services Marketing: People, Technology, Strategy*, 6th Edn., Upper Saddle River, NJ: Prentice Hall.

Rappaport, A. (1986). *Creating Shareholder Value: A Guide for Managers and Investors*, New York: Free Press.

Welch, J. and J. A. Byrne (2001). *Jack: Straight from the Gut*, Business Plus.

4

Performance Management in the Auto Sales Business

Noriyuki Imai
Meijo University

1 Introduction

In the early 1980s, when Japan notably overtook the U.S. in industrial competitiveness and the latter started to reassess its management methods, the business administration and managerial accounting of Japanese automakers — Toyota in particular — drew much attention. "Taking a cue from the Japanese auto industry" was a trend that subsequently spread from the U.S. to all around the world. Banners with the word "Quality" written in bold were hung in factories all across the U.S., while quality control (QC) circles were created and the seven tools of quality control began to be incorporated in the workplace. These efforts, however, all tended to "take a cue from the Japanese auto industry" in terms of competitiveness in manufacturing. Rather than simply denoting the individual work function of manufacturing, however, today's corporate competitiveness denotes the competitiveness inherent in the so-called "inter-company network" that comprises the value chain as a whole, which also includes manufacturing.

From this perspective, this chapter describes the Japanese auto sales industry, particularly performance management at Toyota dealerships. Despite being one of the integral elements in the competitiveness of the Japanese auto industry, this area has not been the focus of much attention until now.

2 Outline of Toyota's Auto Dealerships in Japan

Toyota is one of the world's foremost automakers, producing 7.5 million vehicles in 27 countries and regions and selling them in over 170 countries worldwide. Since its establishment in Japan in 1937, the company has expanded in tandem with Japanese economic growth to lead the motorization of Japan. Presently, Toyota sells approximately two million vehicles in Japan, making it the largest automaker in the country. Two of the driving forces that enabled Toyota to secure its place atop the Japanese market include the company's aggressive development of and investment in new technologies and products attuned to the changing business environment, and the robust network of dealerships that Toyota has created. This chapter provides an outline of Toyota's auto dealerships in Japan, which are the source of the company's exceptional selling ability.

2.1 *Channel system*

Toyota's auto dealership system is composed of two brands and five channels: Toyota, Toyopet, Corolla, and Netz channels, which carry Toyota brand vehicles, and the Lexus channel, which carries the Lexus brand. Toyota sells over 70 vehicle models in Japan through these five channels. These models fall into one of two categories: dedicated models sold through only one channel and models sold through multiple channels.

The system comprises approximately 290 dealerships: approximately 50 in both the Toyota and Toyopet channels, 70 in the Corolla channel, and 120 in the Netz channel. The Lexus channel, on the other hand, is not composed of independent companies; companies that carry the Toyota brand also open stores that carry the Lexus brand models. Toyota and its dealerships enter into agency contracts with one another; that is, the dealerships sell Toyota vehicles to Toyota customers based on Toyota's business strategy in accordance with the terms of the agency contract.

2.2 *Capital structure*

Another characteristic of Japanese Toyota dealerships is their usage of local capital. The Toyota, Toyopet, Corolla, and Netz channels were established in 1946, 1955, 1961, and 1967, respectively. At each point, Toyota recruited influential local investors in each prefecture with the interest of gaining exposure to the auto sales industry. By encouraging these investors to set up auto dealership companies, Toyota built up a robust network of dealerships.

As such, Toyota's directly controlled companies (i.e., subsidiaries) own approximately only 10% and companies run by local investors own approximately 90% of dealership capital. Considering other competitors,

Nissan's subsidiaries own approximately 35% and local companies own approximately 65% of Nissan dealerships, while Honda's subsidiaries and local investors each own approximately 50% of Honda dealerships.

2.3 *Number of stores and employees*

Toyota's auto dealerships in Japan number approximately 5,800 in total: 1,200 in the Toyota channel, 1,200 in the Toyopet channel, 1,500 in the Corolla channel, 1,700 in the Netz channel, and 200 in the Lexus channel (all figures are approximations). Of these, approximately 85% are new vehicle dealerships. There is also a total of approximately 115,000 dealership employees in Japan: 25,000 in the Toyota channel, 27,000 in the Toyopet channel, 30,000 in the Corolla channel, 30,000 in the Netz channel, and 3,000 in the Lexus channel (all figures are approximations). Approximately 39,000 of these employees are new vehicle sales staff and 33,000 are service engineers.

3 The Japanese Auto Sales Business Model

As previously stated, the motorization of Japan grew in tandem with Japanese economic growth. Stated differently, the auto industry is one of Japan's leading industries and the auto sales business is a key driver of the medium- to long-term growth of the Japanese economy. It was against this backdrop that the traditional business model of the Japanese auto sales industry was born and became firmly established. That is, companies created and actively promoted the business model in which the managers at each dealership set high yearly, monthly, and individual sales objectives (quotas) for their sales teams and secured revenue for their dealerships by firmly demanding that their team meet these goals. This can be called the "push" business model, as dealership sales staff are assigned sales objectives (quotas) and drive potential customers to purchase automobiles.

This traditional business model worked rather effectively during the high, stable growth period in Japan during the 1980s but gradually exposed its limitations after the bubble economy burst in the 1990s and Japan entered a period of moribund economic growth. Specifically, under the push model, situations in which sales staff are unable to meet their quotas will occur frequently, leading to a decline in dealership retention rates. Given the unique nature of long replacement cycles inherent in automobiles, this posed a threat to the medium- and long-term selling ability of dealerships.

Here, in keeping with the changing management environment and in line with the principles of the Toyota Production System (TPS) — the main source of the company's competitiveness — as well as its unique systems, Toyota developed and implemented a new auto sales business model, the "pull" model, beginning in the 1990s. The concepts of this model are detailed below.

4   Toyota's Japanese Dealerships and TPS

The first key element of the new pull business model is the introduction of TPS into the distribution and service units of Toyota's Japanese dealerships. These activities are referred to as Toyota sales logistics (TSL) and comprise education and training on the principles of TPS and the practice of *kaizen* based on the special characteristics of the TPS system.

4.1   *Education and training*

Beginning in the 1990s, Toyota leadership, focusing mainly on the distribution and service units of the company's Japanese dealerships, conducted intense education and training on the principles of TPS outlined below. From this training, TPS principles penetrated deeply all the way from Toyota to Toyota's dealerships, creating the groundwork for implementing *kaizen*, based on the uniqueness of TPS system.

(1) Customer first

- Continuously keep in mind the principle of "customer first, dealership second, maker third".

(2) Just in time (JIT)

- Continuously keep in mind the principles of "the required thing at the required time in the required amount", and "do not do or allow anything not required".

(3) *Jidoka*

- Build quality into the production process by creating a mechanism in which machinery (work) automatically stops whenever trouble (irregularity) occurs.

(4) Thoroughly eliminating the "seven wastes"
- Eliminate overproduction waste, waiting time waste, transportation waste, overprocessing waste, inventory waste, action waste, and trouble-creating waste.

(5) *Genchi genbutsu*
- When promoting *kaizen* or work standardization, the most basic approach should be not to accept anything on faith, hold no preconceptions, spend adequate time observing the situation on the ground with your own senses, get a firm grasp, and understand the situation and discover the truth.

(6) Creating a culture for promoting *kaizen*
- Organizations instinctually attempt to cover up problems in order to perpetuate themselves. This instinct needs to be transformed to create an organizational culture in which irregularities and problems are noticeable — that is, a culture in which the concept of *Jidoka* is firmly established.

(7) Respect for people
- People who work at companies spend the majority of the most important time of their lives at the workplace.
- Therefore, making people who work under you spend this important time on unnecessary work amounts to disrespecting that person's life.
- The duty of management supervisors is to make the products and work that these people have spent precious hours of their lives creating valuable.

4.2 *Practice of* Kaizen

Building on the education and training on TPS principles explained earlier, a variety of *kaizen* activities based on the unique qualities of the TPS system are practiced at the distribution, service, and other units of Toyota's Japanese dealerships. Below are two typical examples:

(1) *Kaizen* in the new vehicle delivery process
Whenever a customer orders a new vehicle at a dealership, this order information is routed to Toyota via the dealership headquarters. In accordance with the TPS process, to meet the expected delivery date, Toyota then produces the vehicle according to order and ships it to

the dealer in the shortest lead time possible. After optional components are installed, the car is washed and new vehicle inspection is completed at the dealership's new vehicle service center. The registration process is then completed at the store and the vehicle is finally delivered to the customer. This type of new vehicle delivery process in which work flows from the dealership outlet to dealership headquarters, then to Toyota, then to the dealership's new vehicle center and finally back to the dealership outlet has been subject to several problems. Specifically, (1) the system was divided between the dealerships and Toyota, (2) JIT flow was not present in the processes within the new vehicle centers, and as a result, (3) the total lead time between the customer's order and delivery of the vehicle averaged over a month, and customers could only be notified of the expected delivery time directly before it occurred. *Kaizen* was therefore made within the TSL in which the systems of Toyota and the dealerships were synchronized within the order-delivery process and waste was thoroughly eliminated within the dealership's new vehicle center process, which was transformed as JIT flow. This resulted in far shorter total lead times (from order to delivery to the customer) of around 20 days on average, and customers could now be notified of the expected delivery date before Toyota shipped the vehicle to the dealership. This *kaizen* boosted productivity in the service unit and greatly enhanced customer satisfaction.

(2) *Kaizen* in the vehicle maintenance process

Along with financial services such as installment loans and insurance sales, maintenance services such as inspections and repairs are also a valuable profit center to Toyota's dealership management in Japan. The maintenance process within dealerships' service shops, however, had very long lead times as a whole and varied significantly from shop to shop. Here, Toyota implemented *kaizen* in TSL. Refinements were made to standardized maintenance working times, and tools were introduced into service shops to make work progress management more visible. Service engineers also received training in multiple work functions, creating a new system in which service shops could flexibly and independently give and receive support. This led to shorter and more even lead times in the maintenance process, and considerably improved customer satisfaction. In addition, customer complaints could be conveyed rapidly from the dealership to Toyota through the network connecting dealership service shops, dealership headquarters and Toyota. Toyota could then quickly identify the cause of the complaint, and promptly redesign their products, revise assembly procedures, change the way they procure components, or take other steps to remedy the problem. This framework was constructed through cooperation between the dealership and Toyota.

These are just a few typical examples of TSL that *kaizen* practices at Toyota's Japanese auto dealerships. Toyota unveiled its strategy to further accelerate the adoption of TPS in these dealerships by establishing the "TSL College" in 2009.

5 Management Quality at Toyota's Japanese Auto Dealerships

The second key element of the new pull business model in the auto sales industry is the introduction of the management quality concept into the sales units at Toyota's Japanese auto dealerships. As previously explained, the traditional business model of the Japanese auto sales industry was the push model, in which managers at each dealership set high yearly, monthly, and individual sales objectives (quotas) for their sales teams, and secured revenue for their dealerships by firmly demanding that their team meet these goals.

It was also pointed out that this model gradually exposed its limitations as Japanese economic growth began to stagnate in the 1990s, leading to a decline in auto dealership staff retention rates. Toyota responded to this changing management environment by conceptualizing and implementing new sales strategies. It made pricing clearer by revamping the discount practice, shifted its selling method from visit-based sales to store-based sales, relocated and refurbished dealerships according to changes in the market area, strengthened collaboration between the sales and service divisions within dealerships, and introduced the award system and field days for all of its dealership sales staff.

While these strategies were effective to an extent, the key to a successful transition from the traditional push model to the pull model was how to transform the way in which staff in the sales units of Toyota's auto dealerships worked. A new initiative conceived against this backdrop was the introduction of the management quality concept into the sales units of Toyota's Japanese auto dealerships.

The concept of management quality was developed in the U.S. during the mid-1980s, when the limitations of the push-style mass production method caused the decline in the competitiveness of the manufacturing industry, as a way to restore America's economic advantage. The essence of this concept can be observed specifically in the principles of the Malcolm Baldrige National Quality Award (MB award), which was founded through its legislation in 1987 in the U.S. The MB award recognized companies that had management systems which fulfilled all the quality requirements that an exceptional management should fulfil — going beyond common perspectives on product quality to consider aspects such as customer orientation, human resource orientation, process management and knowledge management — awarding them as a company with exceptional quality management (Hertz, 2000).

Such a concept of management quality, which, much like TPS, pursues organizational excellence with a focus on customers and employees on the principle of respect for people, is the concept that drove the transition of Toyota's auto dealership business model to the pull model. One groundbreaking, leading-edge example of this is the efforts of Netz Toyota Nangoku, Inc. (N Nangoku) introduced here.

5.1 *History and outline*

N Nangoku is a dealership in the Netz channel that carries the Toyota brand product line and was established in 1980 by influential local investors. Presently, N Nangoku has 48 million yen in capital, employs approximately 130 people and generates revenue of approximately five billion yen a year. Operating mainly out of three stores within its home territory of Kochi prefecture, the company's core activities include new car sales, used car purchases and sales, maintenance services spanning all aftercare, and agency operations for property and casualty insurance and telecommunications. Since its establishment, N Nangoku has adopted a management quality concept where "The company, based on the philosophy of respect for people, will first pursue employee satisfaction, then, building on this, employees will continuously pursue customer satisfaction out of their collective will." Based on this concept, the company has designated the construction of a mechanism for creating the value that customers demand as management's highest priority, and consistently promotes organizational operations that revolve around "wowing the customer".

Despite the fact that N Nangoku is an auto dealership, it breaks away completely from the traditional way of selling cars, such as opening several stores and using sales staff visits to scout out potential customers.

By developing high-quality service in the showrooms of its three wide-region stores, the company has consistently achieved top class customer satisfaction among Toyota's Japanese dealerships.

5.2 *Details of the management quality concept*

The management quality concept at N Nangoku is based on Masaru Kamata's personnel development strategy theory, Frederick Herzberg's motivation-hygiene theory, and Abraham Maslow's hierarchy of needs.

Kamata identifies the historically advanced Japanese educational system as one of the drives of the long period of Japanese economic growth and the strong competitiveness of Japanese firms. He then expounds on the importance of human resource development strategy in Japanese firms' overall management strategy going into the 21st century. Specifically, he encouraged a transition from traditional education that directly and unquestioningly incorporated western knowledge, technology, and know-how to a higher-level personnel development system that cultivates workers that seek out know-why — in other words, meaning, purpose and essence — and create their own know-how. Kamata argued that Japanese firms should develop worker creativity and reinforce their competitiveness by shifting to such a system (Kamata, 1984).

In putting Kamata's personnel development strategy theory into practice, N Nangoku focused on the visibility and invisibility of the elements of motivation inherent in Herzberg's motivation-hygiene theory and Maslow's hierarchy of needs. In his motivation-hygiene theory, Herzberg indicated company policies and management, supervisory practices, relationships with superiors, relationships with co-workers, and working conditions as factors that inhibit employee work motivation, and achievement, approval, the work itself, and responsibility as factors that encourage employee work motivation. One can argue that the former tends to be visible factors while the latter tends to be invisible (Herzberg, 1959). In his hierarchy of needs, Maslow puts physiological subsistence and safety and security at the lower levels, and group belonging, self-esteem, and self-actualization at the higher levels. Here, again, the former tends to be highly visible while the latter tends to be much less visible (Maslow, 1965).

Armed with this knowledge, N Nangoku focused on the importance of the invisible factors that increase motivation and worked to improve management quality by making these things as visible (e.g., putting them into words or numbers) as possible. Put differently, more so than highly visible (i.e., easily manageable), elements such as company performance, personal work performance, wages/salary, and promotion, the company ventured to make highly invisible (i.e., generally hard to manage) management elements such as employee satisfaction, customer satisfaction, personal growth through work, acceptance by and trust of those around oneself, and contribution to society the crux of business management.

Sales staff and other employees at N Nangoku are thus instilled with a multifaceted human ability (e.g., perceptiveness, ability to discover problems, creativity, communication, leadership, and management), the value that customers demand is continuously created, and organizational operations revolve around "wowing the customer". Through this, the concept of management quality becomes a reality, and the auto sales industry pull model is realized.

5.3   *Examples of application of the management quality concept*

As stated earlier, N Nangoku's concept of management quality boils down to creating a system for and conducting activities to increase employee satisfaction to realize "a worthwhile workplace and high customer satisfaction achieved by employees who think". Some specific instances in which this concept is applied are explained below.

First is developing strong leadership in order to create new customer value. N Nangoku has proclaimed an entirely new business approach unbound by existing auto sales industry concepts in which "profits are made not by depending on new car sales, but by creating a value chain and securing a stable revenue stream", and "maximizing the satisfaction of employees and existing customers". Under the strong leadership of the president, the company and all of its employees deeply share the same sense of values.

Second is developing unique marketing that seeks to maximize customer satisfaction. In addition to the usual sales activity, N Nangoku integrated customer service counters in its showrooms and is also thoroughly involved in multifaceted sales activities based on the customer card system. The company has a base that can make full use of the customer information gained from these activities, and for many years it has conducted marketing activities based on a unique way of thinking where the company "expands the nature of its relationship with customers".

N Nangoku also strives to communicate with customers at a variety of different contact points such as through the internet, events, and questionnaires in order to collect and understand customer requests, comments, and complaints. In addition, sales staff, service engineers, and showroom staff work quickly and closely together on site during showroom negotiations to deliver a high level of customer satisfaction. Third is practising employee-oriented management that aims to enhance employee "perception" and "create a worthwhile workplace". N Nangoku works to create a culture of "perception" and "thinking" by formulating strategies and conducting project activities with the participation of all employees.

N Nangoku also conducts employee-oriented management that encourages employee autonomy and independence and a desire to contribute in order to "create a worthwhile workplace". It does so by establishing a recognition and compensation system based on the outcome of one's activities, strategic human resource placement, and recruitment of extraordinary employees, among other things.

As a result of these activities, when N Nangoku conducted an internal employee satisfaction survey, employees gave the company extremely high marks in the areas of "ideal personal growth as a person" and "work fulfilment and sense of satisfaction". The results of these applications of the management quality concept have been highly praised, and N Nangoku received the Japan Quality Award in 2002.

6 Business Model and Performance Management at Toyota's Japanese Auto Dealerships

This chapter discussed two different business models in the Japanese auto sales industry: the traditional push model, in which sales staff are required to hit high sales targets (quotas), and the new pull model implemented at Toyota's Japanese dealerships, which melds TPS principles and unique system qualities to improve processes and management quality.

As previously indicated, rather than using the traditional financial and quantitative indicators such as company and individual sales performance, the new pull business model makes non-financial and qualitative indicators such as on-site process lead times, delivery date compliance rates, work quality, productivity, and employee and customer satisfaction the crux of business management.

Considering this from the aspect of performance management in the auto sales industry, in the traditional push model, period profit and sales targets were generally set vertically according to division and individual, and managers conducted performance management through top-down control to meet these targets. While this was generally effective, as explained earlier, in the new pull business model, which emphasizes bottom-up, horizontal collaboration throughout the entire organization, inevitably some ingenuity is required in performance management methods.

There are two different modes of management within the new pull business model. The vertical mode measures achievement of period profit and/or sales objectives under the guidance of headquarters. The horizontal mode pursues on-site–led process improvement and management quality, captures the profit improvement resulting from such a mode, and links this to the period profit management conducted by headquarters. The pull model seeks to organically integrate these two modes into one Dual-mode Management Accounting administrative system (Imai, 2010).

7 Conclusion

The new research area of service science is showing signs of becoming a major field under the following thought (Fujikawa, 2010). Specifically, service science examines the service that has traditionally somewhat relied on experience-based decision-making from a scientific perspective and seeks to systemize this study as a new academic field that blends the social and natural sciences. Research topics in service science are not limited to just the service industry; rather, they combine goods and services based on a new way of looking at services and a new concept of value. This new way of looking at services does not separate them from goods but rather considers all economic activity as services. It further divides them into "services that accompany goods" and "services that do not accompany goods".

The new concept of value within service science is not limited to just the "value exchange" that occurs when products or services are purchased, but emphasizes the "usage value" and "context value" that is realized within the context of the firm and the customer having a mutual effect on each other both before and after the purchase. From this perspective, the performance management of Toyota's Japanese auto dealerships examined here is more than just an example of management in the Japanese service industry. It can be considered, rather, as a groundbreaking and leading-edge example of service science in which the two functions of products and services are organically integrated through the medium of the TPS pull business model.

References

Fujikawa, Y. (2010). Research progress in "service science", *Nihon Keizai Shimbun*, November 18, 2010 (in Japanese).

Hertz, H. S. (2000). *Criteria for Performance Excellence: Malcolm Baldrige National Quality Program, 2001*, Darby, PA: Diane Publishing Co.

Herzberg, F. (1959). *Motivation to Work*, 2nd edn., Hoboken, NJ: John Wiley & Sons.

Imai, N. (2010). The proposal of dual-mode management accounting model: Aiming at the dissolution of "accounting lag", *The Meijo Review*, 10(4), 61–87 (in Japanese).

Kamata, M. (1984). *Employee Education and Techniques for Developing Exceptional Personnel*, Tokyo: Seikei Research Institute, Inc. (in Japanese).

Maslow, A. H. (1965). *Eupsychian Management*, Homewood, IL: Richard D Irwin.

5

Productivity Improvement of Service Business Based on the Human Resource Development: Application of Toyota Production System to the Insurance Firm

Shino Hiiragi

University of Tokyo

1 Introduction

It is a well-known fact that the productivity of the Japanese service sector is quite low compared to the global standard (Ministry of Economy, Trade and Industry, 2007). The thought process typically employed in the Japanese manufacturing sector — the successful application which Japan is universally acknowledged for — is being looked upon as one way to improve this shortfall in productivity (*ibid.*; Levitt, 1972; Looy *et al.*, 2003; Kawada, 2011).

A major advantage of the Japanese manufacturing industry is believed to be its "organizational capability" at the production workplace (*Genba*), which not only supports complexity, but is also consistent with "integral product architecture" (Fujimoto, 2007). Production or manufacturing may be considered as a transfer of design information from the process onto the product. A pioneering study in the field (Sato and Fujimoto, 2007) suggests that this "open (or wide sense) concept" in the manufacturing arena may also be theoretically applicable to the non-manufacturing industry, namely service industries.

Numerous studies have focused on well-known Japanese manufacturing companies such as Toyota, Panasonic, and Kyocera in Japan (Ogawa, 1994; Satake, 1998; Hino, 2005; Fujimoto, 1999; Hiki, 2007; Hiiragi, 2009; Kawada, 2009; Nakase, 2009; Amoeba Management Research Study Meeting, 2010;

Monden, 2011; Wang, 2011). In their attempt to theorize the management systems at the subject companies, there are some studies to bring about an introduction to and understanding of various concepts such as the "knowledge creation company theory" (Nonaka and Takeuchi, 1995), the "autonomous organization system" (Hiromoto, 2005), and "dynamic influence management (DIM)" (Oku *et al.*, 2011).

However, the Toyota Production System (TPS) is the most well-known and best studied of its counterparts even in other countries except Japan (Senge *et al.*, 2000; Liker, 2004; Liker and Meier, 2005; Rother, 2010). However, TPS is a theory and may not be applicable in the real world. Even if a company imitates only Kanban, it cannot become Toyota. In this case, the importance of human resource development and capacity building cannot be overemphasized.

The knowledge of the human resource development theory has been traditionally confined to the field of education (psychology, to be precise). In business though, it has tended to be more of a practice rather than a theory. In this chapter, I intend to critically explore whether human resource development as practiced in the manufacturing sector can translate into a useful methodology for service industries, and how this may be possible. Specifically, I will inspect how the approach adopted by the manufacturing industry may be introduced with a view to improve productivity in the service sector. To this end, I shall examine a case study where TPS was introduced in an office environment.

2   Contribution of TPS Toward Productivity Improvement

In this chapter, I shall provide the explanation of the term "productivity", and bring out how TPS can contribute toward productivity improvement.

2.1   *Explanation of the term "productivity" and how productivity improvement realization can become a problem*

In 2007, industry and research institutions commenced an official collaboration titled *Service Productivity and Innovation for Growth* on the study and improvement of productivity in Japanese service industries. Ministry of Economy, Trade and Industry (2007) report states,

> Service industries are extremely important industries that account for almost 70% of the Japanese economy, whether

measured in terms of GDP or employment. .... While the role of service industries is increasing, its rate of productivity growth is relatively low when compared to domestic manufacturing industry or service industries in other countries. Thus, achieving innovation and productivity improvement in service industries is an important agenda for the development of the Japanese economy.

In general, productivity is expressed in terms of a ratio. This ratio is denoted by the total output (numerator) divided by the total input (denominator). The extent of improvement in productivity is gauged by the increase in the measure of output per unit input. An important point to remember here is that productivity is not equivalent to efficiency. It is concerned with both of "increasing value added/creating new business" and "improving efficiency". An illustration in the Ministry of Economy, Trade and Industry report says the difference between these two terms as follows;

To improve productivity in service industries, it is important to (1) pursue efficiency and (2) improve service quality such as improving customer satisfaction and hospitality. .... In addition, efforts in such areas as cultivating human resources are considered effective for both efficiency and quality improvement (*ibid.*).

In this report, not only the reducing input as a denominator but also increasing output as a numerator is weighted heavily. And it shows the viewpoint that value-added improvement of the output comes about not just through service quality improvement but also through creation of new business and innovation. Furthermore, it says that all of them occur under the human development.

The report is based on the extensive opinion collection from the spot of the service industry of Japan. So I think that proposal is to be notable point of view when the profitability of the services is discussed. In this chapter, these three improvement of efficiency, value-added (service quality), and human development will be focused.

2.2   *The advantage conferred by the "man" of 4Ms (Man, Machine, Material, Method) on the Japanese manufacturing industry*

Efficient process management at the production workplace is no doubt the hallmark of the Japanese manufacturing industry. This is equivalent to the "design transcription" element in the "design transcription theory". Japan rates quite strongly in the successful implementation of the "Method" component of the 4Ms (Man, Machine, Material, Method) framework of production control, which in turn facilitates the successful management of the other 3Ms. While all 3M elements affect process management mutually, the human element is particularly important. Interestingly, TPS is a good representative example to the effect.

2.3 Human resource development: A characteristic of TPS in process management

Following World War II, faced by a lack of resources in particular, the Japanese manufacturing industry revitalized itself through various improvements. In particular, employees were encouraged to be part of the production process. Jointly, these various improvements led to the birth of TPS. Thereafter, TPS continued to evolve in periods of better economic growth (Hiiragi, 2009). In TPS, the most significant effects on process value delivery are achieved by designing a process capable of delivering the required results smoothly. This way of thinking is also applicable to the service industries.

3 Application of TPS to the Service Industries — A Case Study

In this chapter, I shall examine a case of TPS introduction in the back-office of an insurance firm.

The principles of TPS were introduced at a life insurance company (henceforth referred to as Company A). Company A initiated activities to introduce the manufacturing industry approach in its back-office. The experiment commenced in March 2009 and continued till October 2011. Given that the concept and principles were entirely new to Company A, the guidance of an external consultant (Company B) in "*kaizen*" (continuous improvement) project (PJ) was provided at the outset. After PJ, the employees became confident about participating in group discussions and providing inputs related to their workplace environment. In addition, in all group companies, the section in charge of promotions was organized.

The outcomes of this entire exercise were analyzed in April 2011, mainly through a two-hour-long interview with Mr. X, the management representative of the process improvements department. In addition, four key participants (three guidance trainers and one project coordinator) of the external consultant (Company B) were also interviewed on more than a dozen occasions during this experiment. The analysis was further supplemented by documents detailing PJ, made by Company B.

3.1 *Significance of employing a manufacturing industry approach in the back-office of an insurance company*

It is important to appreciate the need for applying a manufacturing industry approach such as the TPS to an insurance company. In order to do this, we need to consider the product properties of life insurance in general, and understand the background of Company A in particular.

The following is a short outline of Company A.

- One of the largest life insurance companies in Japan.
- Capital: 201,200 million yen.
- Total assets: 30,869,600 million yen.
- Insurance revenue: 3,056,500 million yen.
- Claims paid or payable: 2,625 billion yen (as of March 31, 2011).
- Affiliate businesses: Eighteen national companies, 11 overseas companies.
- Employees: 56,908 people (Back-office: 13,381, Insurance sales: 43,527).
- Management policy: "Always value the customer".

Company A came up with an Initial Public Offering (IPO) in April 2009, and was listed on the Tokyo Stock Exchange. Company A therefore also faces an ongoing requirement to disclose financial and business information.

When asked why Company A decided to opt for an approach in the manufacturing industry for its back-office operations, Mr. X said,

> In the autumn of 2008, we examined ways and means to reinforce our working systems, primarily as a consequence of the Company being listed on the stock exchange. In the past, our company concentrated mainly on providing diverse product offerings, matched by an efficient sales system. However, we also felt the necessity to strengthen our back-office operations, so as to make our company more cost competitive.

To that end, Company A decided to empower its employees toward pinpointing and implementing suggestions for improving their workplace, and thus reinforcing their competitiveness. This led to the introduction of TPS. It was referred to as the "manufacturing industry approach".

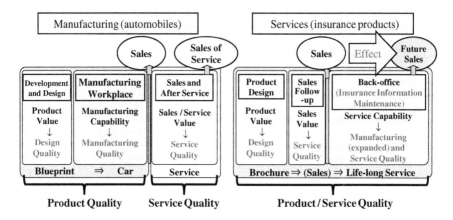

Fig. 1. The difference of the quality structure in the manufacturing (car) and services (insurance products).
Source: Author, based on Company C document.

Here, the fact that Company A chose to employ such an approach for a back-office is significant. Typically, there is no customer interface at this end. Additionally, the nature of life insurance products is such that the pay-out does not take place till the end of the insurance term, which can occur many years following the sale of the policy. This differs to a great extent from the product delivery process in the manufacturing industry (Fig. 1).

3.2   Improvement in process flow (Method 1): efficiency improvement through improved time management

A *kaizen* PJ of Company A was performed over five phases for two years and eight months. The target workplaces were the company's back-office work center, another main office, the information processing units which were part of the group subsidiary, and its distribution channel. The first activity focused on streamlining major work elements at the back-office, one of the more vital being the maintenance (management and correction when required) and processing of insurance details of the insured parties. Implementing this change brought about a marked improvement in the process flow; the time delay or stagnancy in work related to documentation was removed, thus bringing about an improvement in efficiency.

However, there is the question of how one may measure production per unit time. In TPS, the first basic unit time is measured, which in turn helps decide the work cycle time. With this in mind, based on the cycle, an overall production progress schedule is planned and executed. The results help to differentiate the total planned duration of the process from its actual run time, and thereby provide leads on how the work may be completed in a more efficient way.

For the office workplace environment also, it was necessary to decide on a basic unit of measurement to begin with. However, this was not easy given that a measurable numerical value may not necessarily exist for such an environment. However, a reasonably experienced person does have a fairly clear understanding as to the processing time taken for a particular type of document, or the number of sheets according to the degree of difficulty, and so on. Based on these inputs, the typical duties for an employee in such an office environment were classified into the type of document (three kinds), the type of work processes (four processes), and the degree of processing difficulty (three classifications). Using the resulting combinations, a unit of time was assumed to belong to one of the 72 kinds of standard time units.

A confounding factor was a bias that could be introduced by conditions such as the deficient or incomplete documentation, which would increase the actual processing time. This was solved by ensuring that documentation was processed in small lots. Then, a visualization of the flow of documents by tray unit was performed. A document progress management array was prepared to help sort each process and the time required for the same by length and breadth. The employee was therefore well informed about the next work item in the process. It became possible to identify all leads and lags in the work process at first sight. A specially developed Microsoft Excel model helped this visualization.

As a result of these developments, processing time per document improved by approximately 15% one year after the manufacturing industry approach was introduced at Company A (Nikkei Information Strategy, 2010). Such an accomplishment this early on was highly appreciated by the management at Company A. In the second phase of implementation, the approach was introduced at a new location, and it met with the same success as its predecessor. Indeed, it has become the accepted standard of practice for paperwork in Company A.

3.3   *Improvement in process flow (Method 2): preventing mistakes and quality improvement by the work standardization*

One of the reasons for the introduction of the manufacturing industry approach was to stabilize the quality of back-office work done through the standardization of the work process and to prevent mistakes. Therefore, ways of thinking such as "standardization", "own process conclusion", and "true reason pursuit" were introduced in the manufacturing industry.

Details of all the work at the production workplace were recorded, and prescribed as standard work. The requisite details were then listed in documents such as operational procedures, which were always referred to by a worker. Induction training for new employees was also conducted based on these documents.

Company A had already documented its work manuals and the flowcharts before introducing the manufacturing industry approach. However, this time the manuals and original flowcharts were documented by employees in charge of the concerned duties after joint discussions amongst themselves. This effort highlighted the choice of the most rational and efficient methods in detail, which could be easily replicated by an employee really new to that process.

In the event a mistake occurred, it became imperative to analyze the reasons for the same. The Standardize-Do-Check-Act or SDCA cycle of continuous improvement (Fig. 2) can be an invaluable way in this regard

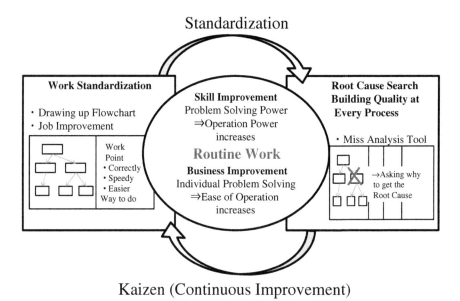

Fig. 2.   Mutual relations of "the work standardization" and "the improvement by Miss true reason pursuit" in the office work.
Source: Author, based on Company B document.

by using these tools. As a result of the application of the PJ, the number of errors in document processing per year decreased to approximately one-third of the original number (Nikkei Information Strategy, 2010).

3.4 *Significance of the human resource improvement in the company — The simultaneous achievement of efficiency and quality improvement*

The analysis of the above two effects is not as straightforward as it seems. It is fairly evident that processing time and overtime were reduced as a result of the application of time management. Over time however, (within more than two and a half years of Company A starting to apply this approach), the core of that PJ was revealed to be the flowcharting of work processes. This element undoubtedly deserves our attention. While flowcharts were initially employed as a means to help reduce work errors, to make the employee positive and competent through PJ, they eventually became the very foundation of the manufacturing industry approach in Company A.

In general, quality improvement is not entirely compatible with efficiency improvement. There is some amount of trade-off involved. Therefore, in order to enable a workplace to pursue quality and efficiency at the same time, it becomes important to reinforce its ability for improvement. Indeed, constant improvement becomes the driving force for pursuing efficiency and quality simultaneously, as depicted by the change from α to β in Fig. 3.

This aspect was not originally a consideration when Company A decided to introduce the manufacturing industry approach, but was discovered a bit later. Mr. X said about the discovery,

> We realized and believed the importance of time management early on. However, 3–4 months after introducing the concept, an on-site manager remarked, "The atmosphere of the workplace has changed considerably. The ability of individual employees to conduct work more efficiently is evident." I too made the same observation on other occasions. Then, I noticed that an unprecedented spirit of voluntary and active discussion, identification and enforcement of suggestions made by the employees themselves towards various improvements in work processes. I realized that this was the true advantage of TPS, which often remains unacknowledged. This positive change in the employees' attitude came about as a result of their participation in the making of the

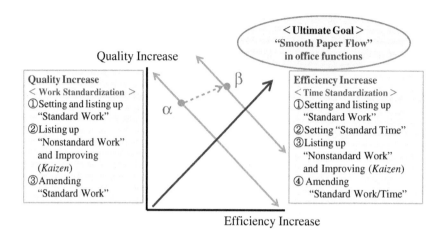

Fig. 3. Trade-off cancellation of efficiency improvement and quality improvement in Company A.

flowchart tools. We thought we would concentrate on preparing the flowcharts first and then put them to practical use. However, I noticed that mere participation in the flowchart preparation exercise helped employees perform their duties better. This was not a one-off occurrence. The effect it had on our employees and their outputs made it our secret weapon against competitors. (April, 2011)

One of the trainers from Company B, who led the PJ said,

I have always believed that work efficiency increases with the introduction of the concept of time management. I also realized that human resource development held the key for the successful future of Company A. Therefore, I consciously planned the training in such a manner that the employees would be able to hone their talents towards using these methods, and making the necessary improvements by themselves. The results from the first model workplace were very encouraging. After making a few adjustments to the initial training plan, we applied it to the next workplace, and I was convinced about its effectiveness when it was much effective there, too. (March, 2010)

Generally, quality and efficiency are recognized to be in binary opposition. However, TPS advocates that they should be balanced and both gained. This is possible only through a capable and empowered human resource; after all, a human only designs the work systems and builds them.

No wonder the popular Japanese saying goes, "manufacturing is made with a person" (own translation).

3.5   Human resource development to enable autonomous organization construction: Manabiai (mutual learning) and autonomous duties improvement

The following observation is often acknowledged as a characteristic of Japanese business management. Employees not only understand the targets assigned to them but also are motivated to enable the company to achieve its goals. Furthermore, deploying the Plan-Do-Check-Act or PDCA cycle of improvement can serve as the MCS (Management Control System) for autonomous organization is enforced all together.

In Company A, this autonomous organization became evident on account of human resource development. The key word that comes to mind here is *Manabiai* (translated as "mutual learning"). Originally, *Manabiai* was applied from a pedagogic viewpoint, as a technique in administering classes in elementary and junior high schools (Nishikawa, 2000). Conventional guidelines mandate that a teacher should make a guidance plan and teach it according to a set procedure. However, in *Manabiai*, while the teaching plan and objectives of the study session are set by a teacher, a considerable part of the learning is accomplished through activities contributed by the student or child. This gives rise to the autonomous learning form, the crux of which lies not in teaching, but in mutual learning.

For Company A, this method was applied to initiate human resource development for adult employees (Fig. 4). The conventional system of one-way interaction between the employee and the supervisor was replaced instead by a discussion-oriented participation, where each employee contributed to the overall goal at hand.

Participation in this activity produced a feeling of ownership of the procedure drawn in the flowchart. The participatory approach allowed each employee to experience a sense of accomplishment, feel confident (self-affirmatory) about their work, and be part of a team and the organization as a whole.

Again, these experiences are not a result of possessing certain knowledge/skill sets. The entire exercise leads to an improvement in employee motivation. Not surprisingly, during the debriefing session of this PJ at

Shino Hiiragi

	Kaizen Method	*Manabiai* (mutual learning)
Team Configu- ration	• Leadership type • Weak interaction among members • Hierarchy	• All-round communication type • Equally distributed relationship • Autonomous
Team Function	Leader drives activity ⇒Leader's big influence	Each person brings one's opinion ⇒Reflecting all members opinion
Leader	Pre-selected Leader ⇒Risk of becoming a flag-person only	Leader is selected naturally ⇒Role allotment / Collaboration
Purpose of the Activity	Display of results for external parties ⇒Risk of undertaking activity for announcements alone	Improvement of the employee's own duties ⇒Gathering everyday opinion of employees
Characte -ristics	Each team must come to a conclusion in the shortest possible time⇒Best Practice	The manner in which an employee undertakes his duties is examined => Each team member can improve
Satis- faction	"I do not want to continue." Leader feels team members are not co-operating. Team members feel that work is forced upon them.	All team members eager to continue the activity. Overall sense of satisfaction and achievement exists.
Kaizen Effect	Improvements may only be temporary. Pace of improvement is restored after the activity.	Team members are constantly aware of need for improvements and do it. Pace of improvements is continuous and increases over time.

Fig. 4.   A comparison between the method of improvement PJ and *Manabiai*. *Source*: Author, based on Company B document.

Company A, a considerable number of employees supported this. The management was of the view that,

> By implementing this action, we have achieved a way to become more competitive throughout our company. We noticed this action helped highlight latent qualities in talented employees. Talented employees with a will (motivation) as well as skills were more easily developed.

Respect for human nature thus forms a crucial part and parcel of TPS or the Toyota way of thinking. Indeed, the concept of *Manabiai* can help both top and bottom hierarchies in organizations. That is a very important point. There is an overwhelming difference between the roles and experience levels, between a teacher and a child (student) in school. However, in spite of these differences in duty and authority, it is ultimately the sense of equality among human beings that counts, and this is true in business also. Viewed in this light, *Manabiai* not only facilitates learning among followers but also allows them to teach and learn interactively between a leader and followers in business.

4 The Specific Significance of the Human Resource Development in the Service Industry: Conclusion and Indications for Future Research

A case was analyzed, where the TPS concept was introduced to an office environment in a service industry. The application of the manufacturing industry approach was fruitful. One important point to remember in this case is that unlike the manufacturing industry (where the majority of the work is done by machines), the employee performs all the work functions for a service industry. This characteristic influenced the uptake of the approach to a huge extent. Here, the significance of the human element in any organizational activity cannot be overemphasized, and developing this resource to enable better work outcomes becomes much more important. In another previous case study, the improvement of the human element was pointed (Sugimoto, 1991).

The activity brought about positive changes in attitudes of employees not just at lower levels but also at the middle and top management layers. They noticed "the latent profit from an employee". As a future goal, Company A should focus on embedding this approach across all levels of the organization. This would be analogous to a strategic reinforcement of the MCS design by centering on human resource development/optimum utilization.

This focus on human resource development and the reinforcement of the conventional information system shall become the two wheels on which the future success of Company A will ride. It must be remembered that this is by no means an individual activity confined to a group or section. Cooperation between the various functions across the organization hierarchy becomes imperative. Provided these aspects are kept in mind, Company A will be able to reinforce its competitiveness to a considerable extent.

In the near future, I would be interested in analyzing a number of examples similar to the theme of this paper and extracting a standard/universal theory that would apply in such instances to all service industries.

Acknowledgments

I would like to thank various people who extended their cooperation toward this study. Mr. X, Management Representative of the Process Improvements Department of Company A, provided his valuable time toward the interview and associated documentation mentioned in this paper. I would also like to express my grateful thanks to the several trainers and staff of TPS consulting Company B, without their assistance and inputs this paper would have been incomplete.

References

Amoeba Management Research Study Meetings (2010). *Amoeba Management Theory and Practice*, Tokyo: KCCS Management Consulting (in Japanese).

Fujimoto, T. (1999). *Evolution Manufacturing System at Toyota*, Oxford: Oxford University Press.

Fujimoto, T. (2007). *Competing to Be Really Really Good: The Behind-the-Scenes Drama of Capability-Building Competition in the Automobile Industry*, Tokyo: I-House Press.

Hiiragi, S. (2009). Accounting suitable for the Toyota Production System: Feasibility of the fair performance evaluation, PhD Dissertation No.7, Aichi Institute of Technology (in Japanese).

Hiki, F. (2007). *Improvement of the Management Accounting — Improvement Process in Japanese Enterprise*, Tokyo: Moriyama-Shoten (in Japanese).

Hino, S. (2005). *Inside the Mind of Toyota: Management Principles for Enduring Growth*, New York, NY: Productivity Press.

Hiromoto, T. (2005). Management accounting system as a micro-macro loop, *The Hitotsubashi Review*, 134(5), 828–858 (in Japanese).

Kawada, M. (ed.) (2009). *Toyota Way-Rio Industrializing Management Accounting for New Age*, Tokyo: Chuokeizai-sha (in Japanese).

Kawada, M. (2011). Toyota way from the viewpoint of the service science, in Kinoshita, E. (ed.), *The Theory and Practice of Service Sciences*, Tokyo: Kindai Kagaku sha, 91–103 (in Japanese).

Levitt, T. (1972). Production-line approach to service, *Harvard Business Review*, September, 50(5), 41–52.

Liker, J. K. (2004). *The Toyota Way*, New York, NY: McGraw-Hill.

Liker, J. K. and D. P. Meier (2005). *The Toyota Way Fieldbook*, New York, NY: McGraw-Hill.

Looy, B. V., P. Gemmel and R. V. Dierdonck (2003). *Services Management: An Integrated Approach*, 2nd edn., Essex: Pearson Education Limited.

Ministry of Economy, Trade and Industry (2007). *Towards Innovation and Productivity Improvement in Service Industries*, Tokyo: Research Institute of Economy, Trade and Industry.

Monden, Y. (2011). *Toyota Production System: An Integrated Approach to Just-in-time*, 4th edn., Cambridge, MA: Taylor & Francis.

Nakase, A. (2009). Restructuring of the management system and creation of a global network by Panasonic, *Keiei Kenkyu (The Commemoration Volume of Prof. K. Yasui, Prof. A. Hata and Prof. H. Kameda)*, 59(4), 187–204 (in Japanese).

Nikkei Information Strategy (2010). 15% Efficiency improvement of paperwork in a way of Toyota (in Japanese), 14 October.

Nishikawa, J. (2000). *Mutual Learning in the Classroom — Learning Clinic Analysis of the Learner as a Teacher, the Teacher as a Producer*, Tokyo: Toyokan Publishing (in Japanese).

Nonaka, I. and H. Takeuchi (1995). *The Knowledge-Creating Company: How Japanese Companies Create the Dynamics of Innovation*, Oxford: Oxford University Press.

Ogawa, E. (ed.) (1994). *A Study of the Toyota Production System*, Tokyo: Nikkei Inc. (in Japanese).

Oku, M., Y. W. Park and S. Hiiragi (2011). Dynamic influence management supporting global competitive advantage — FOA II System supporting DIM —, *MMRC Discussion Paper Series* No. 361 (in Japanese).

Satake, H. (1998). *The Generation, Development, Transformation of Toyota Production System*, Tokyo: Toyo Keizai (in Japanese).

Sato, H. and T. Fujimoto (2007). Attempt at interpretation of the "Monozukuri" approach to the finance business, *Akamon Management Review*, 6(3), 85–116 (in Japanese).

Senge, P. M., H. T. Johnson and A. Broms (2000). *Profit Beyond Measure: Extraordinary Results through Attention to Work and People*, New York, NY: Free Press.

Sugimoto, T. (1991). *Quality Management of Office Work, Sales, and Service (Revised Version)*, Tokyo: Japanese Standards Association (in Japanese).

Rother, M. (2010). *Toyota Kata: Managing People for Improvement, Adaptiveness, and Superior Results*, New York, NY: McGraw-Hill.

Wang, S. (2011). A study on rebuilding the system of strategic cost management at the shop floor, PhD Dissertation (in Japanese).

6

Enacting Entrepreneurial Process on Family Business — Case of Health Care Business

Dun-Hou Tsai
National Sun Yat-sen University, Taiwan

Anders W Johansson
Linnaeus University, Sweden

Shang-Jen Li*
Meiho University, Taiwan

1 Introduction

Economic activity throughout much of the world exhibits a family-related dimension (Morck and Steier, 2005). Many famous and important businesses in the world are family owned, thus the presence of family business in the economic landscape nowadays is quite significant. Researchers and practitioners began to systematically explore the impact of family ownership and management about three decades ago. Many scholars have devoted themselves to this field and thousands of papers concerning discussions on topics such as succession, uniqueness of family business, the effect of family relationship on business and the development of family business research itself have been produced (Sharma, 2004; Casillas and Acedo, 2007). Beneath these themes, entrepreneurship is intertwined and

---

*Corresponding author

highly recognized and pointed. Since family business is easily fixated on a previously successful strategy, it is locked in a fixed business setting, which hampers its further growth. Entrepreneurship provides innovative infusing to family business that bring about creation and change for a positive outperformance.

This chapter uses a narrative approach to represent the recreation of a family business. The main character in the story is the Chinese Clinic Director, Dr. Fu, who was born and raised in a Chinese medical family. His family (grandfather, father, and four sons) is involved in Chinese medicine business and is united by a common tradition but enacts different business paradigms between and within two generations. Fu's father is quite conservative in running their Chinese medical clinic, while his third younger brother is far more proactive when compared with his father. Dr. Fu is influenced by both of these apparent contradictions in his family and has carved his own path of functioning, in which he uses unique, innovative means to conduct Chinese medical chain clinics in Southern Taiwan.

Fu intended to work as a professional doctor in his father's clinic after he graduated from the China Medical College. However, the family was divided as a result of a major conflict between his third younger brother and the father on how a Chinese medical business should be run. Consequently, Fu's three brothers went separate ways and started their own clinics. Then Fu's third brother asked him to be the director of one local hospital. From that point on, the journey of Fu's "entrepreneuring" (Steyaert, 2007) sets off. Fu's story presents his transition from a professional doctor to a clinic director and then to an entrepreneur. It presents the transformation of a family heritage as well. The chapter is built upon three different stories.

The first story tells us how Dr. Fu learnt to manage and conduct a Chinese medical clinic from field work within his daily practice (Schön, 1983). An encounter in a coffee shop is an important part of the plot about how he learnt the way to arrange complex items in the clinic. In what he presented, we can see the capacity of narrative knowing (Bruner, 1986, 1990; Orlikowski, 2002). This story also demonstrates that the emergence of a managerial sense is a process of becoming, rather than an effect of a given personal nature (Giddens, 1991).

The second story is about how Fu established, practiced, and refined his "practical theory" (Rae, 2004) through opening his first clinic "Yi-Fan". This story presents an example of the repetitive process, which goes through the stages of "practice–establishment–refinement–accumulation". Thus Fu built up his personal practical theory from it, which helps Fu to manage his clinics very successfully.

Furthermore, in the third story, Fu proceeded to obtain management education and enrolled in the EMBA program. This program mainly teaches advanced managerial education for businessmen, executives, or higher-ranked managers. Here, Fu met with diverse professional workers, who infused him with many innovative ideas, which were practiced for class discussion. This story presents the process of reinterpretation from imitation to creation (Johansson, 2007). Fu learnt from his classmate's best practices, reflected about situated contexts within his clinics, and then took a more structured way to conduct business management. What he previously managed and conducted is enabled by his reflections and interactions. The institutional education and others' best practices that he imbibed in the EMBA program shed a new light for Fu on how to establish a well-organized yet very innovative construct to advance his business.

2 Innovation, Entrepreneurship, and Narrative Theory

Schumpeter's view of innovation and entrepreneurship has been extremely influential. At its core is bringing the market to disequilibrium by new ways of combining existing resources. The early Schumpeter equated entrepreneurship with innovation, as he proposed that it takes an entrepreneur to undertake destructive creation to bring the market out of equilibrium (Schumpeter, 1934). Furthermore, Knight (1921) focused on the connection between entrepreneur and innovation. He argued that entrepreneurship is a kind of mental trait that an entrepreneur possessed, and those who have such a spirit can endure uncertainty and have initiative enough to exercise self-control and self-efficacy to create the innovations and to earn profit.

The later Schumpeter viewed innovation as a more and more complex phenomenon taking place in a capitalistic system that is becoming gradually more bureaucratic. Therefore the extraordinary entrepreneur was less and less crucial for bringing markets out of disequilibrium as innovation became more and more a collective and calculated phenomenon according to him. Since Schumpeter, the discourses on innovation and entrepreneurship by and large have lived separate lives. Some have focused innovation as a major activity to sustain the ongoing function of today's organization, society and economic system (Drucker, 1995) whereas others have focused on entrepreneurship and sometimes equated entrepreneurship with venture creation (e.g., Gartner, 1985).

In early studies, the formulation of entrepreneurship was viewed from an objectivistic viewpoint presuming a static state and being. Because entrepreneurship was regarded as emphasizing the heroic destructive innovation and as the revolutionary transformation that destructs economic equilibrium (Schumpeter, 1934), entrepreneurship was seen as the innate ability of an individual to opportunity discovery and to create new value by new ventures. Based on this assumption, the themes of previous researches highlighted the entrepreneur's traits such as personality, attribute, psychological cognition, behavioral pattern, and background. As a result, entrepreneurship became the innate privilege of the Great Man.

Although these researchers provided us with some useful understanding about entrepreneurship, they overused given conditions and factors under certain kinds of situation in their research (Shane and Venkataraman, 2000), which cannot completely describe entrepreneurship (Low and MacMillan, 1988; Yamada, 2003). From an "entrepreneuring perspective", Steyaert (2004, 2007) regarded the formulation of entrepreneurship as an individual's social engagements and interactions in facing everyday situations. Therefore, previous understandings of entrepreneurship are on its way to being transformed from emphasizing a single key-person (e.g., entrepreneur) to focusing on the dialogue of the whole entrepreneurial process. Hence, in this chapter we focus on the entrepreneurial process so that entrepreneurship becomes a kind of process that is dynamic and becoming. In other words, entrepreneurship is the result of everyday's actions, which does not belong exclusively to the Great Man (Steyaert, 2004).

As conceptions of entrepreneurship have become more and more diverse, efforts have been made to come back to the core. In one example, Cunningham and Lischeron (1991) tried to conclude what entrepreneurship is, and proposed six different perspectives: great man and psychological, which focused on characteristics of entrepreneur; classic school, which focused on opportunity recognition; managerial and leadership, which focused on entrepreneurial activities and management; and intrapreneurship, which focused on deployment of resources.

Two major elements can be elicited from these six perspectives: (1) the entrepreneur is seen as a core element in entrepreneurship; (2) a focus on temporal stages instead of whole successive processes. Both elements divert the focus on entrepreneurship from the contextual and interactive elements. Low and MacMillan (1988) have identified these shortcomings in entrepreneurial research and proposed that the emphasis should be placed on entrepreneurial process.

However, focus now seems to have been shifted from static characteristic discussion to dynamic process discussion in addressing entrepreneurship even among mainstream entrepreneurship researchers. Shane and Venkataraman (2000) have proposed that entrepreneurship as the nexus of entrepreneur, opportunity, and entrepreneurial process. Based upon such an argument, they have explained how entrepreneurs incorporate their past experiences and learning and then contribute to successful venture creation. Smart and Josephine (1994) argued that entrepreneurship is an ability to detect market opportunity, and moreover, such an ability has to incorporate innovative thought and management skills because then it can contribute to venture creation.

Thus these mainstream scholars have realized the importance of entrepreneurial process in conducting the entrepreneurial research. Nevertheless, they did not elaborate how this process proceeds as well as the content of it. Ucbasaran *et al.* (2001) conveyed corresponding idea with Low and MacMillan(1988) and highlighted the significance of interrelationship among entrepreneur, environment and entrepreneurial activities. Pitt (1998) employed practical theory to analyze entrepreneur's narrative and tried to figure out how entrepreneurial process proceeds. And he found that the motivation comes from entrepreneur's successive sense-making that enables the entrepreneur to carry on his or her venturing. Rae (2000, 2004) based on his conceptual framework to elicit practical theory of entrepreneurs and generalized them into practice-based model. He identified three major stages; family background, prior working experience, and experience in venture creation. These three are important to entrepreneurial learning and venture creation.

It seems that is now again time to reunite innovation and entrepreneurship. In this chapter, we can rely on Drucker (1985) as well as Steyaert (2007) in defining entrepreneurship as "innovation created from daily life engagement and social interaction of individuals". And furthermore, the arguments of Pitt (1998), Rae and Carswell (2001), Rae (2004) and Steyaert (2007) facilitate our elaboration in this chapter.

The notion of practical theory identifies the way in which an individual's knowledge is gained through social interaction and experience. As Rae and Carswell (2001) suggested, personal theory can be shaped by one's experiences from his social life and interaction. Furthermore, Bruner (1990) also indicated that personal theory emerges from an individual's thought and action. People perceive and respond to daily events by referring to their past experience and the best model takes shape from this process. As mentioned earlier, human knowledge comes from daily practices, such as how a kid learns to ride a bicycle. This kind of knowledge is not an objective being but practical wisdom.

As Lave (1988) indicated, practical knowledge is acquired through one's contextual knowing that has a particular setting. Schön (1983) identified how a practitioner reacts in his practical context is mainly based on an action-knowing procedure. This is what Maturana and Varela (1998) have mentioned as "all doing is knowing, and all knowing is doing".

The idea of practical theory can be fruitful ground when it is employed to understand "entrepreneuring". Due to the high velocity and dynamic nature, entrepreneurs act and react to the markets by situated perception. Considering the causality on entrepreneurship is not predetermined, entrepreneurs take action contextually then new enterprises are built through this on-going process. Through the lens of practical theory, we have focused on the entrepreneurial process in which entrepreneurs exercise trial and error, modify, adapt to the market, and finally find what works along this way.

3   Methodology

3.1   *Life story tradition*

The life story approach has its roots in sociology. Since the end of the 1970s, biography research has been enjoying a renaissance (Bertaux and Kohli, 1984; Chamberlayne *et al.*, 2000). An increased interest around life stories and narrative studies can be seen in fields like psychology, psychiatry, psychoanalysis, anthropology, education, literature, and philosophy. In entrepreneurship research, narrative approaches and story-telling have become quite popular (*cf.* special issue of *Journal of Business Venturing,* 2007, p. 5) However, case studies of families and social processes in its fuller sense, as exemplified in Chamberlayne *et al.* (2000), are still almost missing in the field of entrepreneurship.

In order to qualify as life story approach, Bertaux and Kohli (1984, p. 217) argues that research should be based on narratives about one's life or relevant parts thereof. Life stories are something that relates to the totality of a person's experiences. This totality can be elicited in a number of different ways as there are many ways of talking about one's past as well as the interaction between a researcher and a narrator can take different routes. In this chapter, the narrator/entrepreneur has been involved extensively in the beginning phases of the research process in a quite unique way when compared to other entrepreneurship studies. While narrative approaches have been used in entrepreneurship research, life stories only now and then have been articulated. Martyn Pitt and David Rae are among the few who make explicit use of the concept life stories while. Of these two, only Pitt discusses the methodological side in any depth as well as relating more clearly to the life story approach as described by Bertaux and Kohli or other biographical research.

Before we describe in more detail the research process used in this chapter, we will give a brief account of the life story of Dr. Fu and his family as to how it connects to the running of Chinese Medical clinics.

Dr. Fu was born in a Chinese medical family. His father ran a conventional Chinese medical clinic and hired his four children to serve there. Since Fu's father received traditional Chinese medical training, he was satisfied with having a local mid-sized clinic, which involved the whole family. However, his sons did not agree with his conservative mindset, especially Geo, who is Fu's third younger brother. Geo had tried to convince his father to give him a chance to establish a branch where he could be in charge. The two of them quarreled over this issue for a long time.

Fu was different from his three younger brothers. What he wanted was to be a resident doctor at his father's clinic. Nevertheless, Geo tried to convince Fu to run their own business together and expand their father's clinic. The conflict between Geo and his father was so fierce that Geo separated from his father and started his own clinic. Two years later, Geo owned two clinics and invited Fu to manage one of them. Since Geo quarreled with his father, Fu had been through a tough time staying at his father's clinic because he could not accept his style in various ways. For this reason, Fu felt forced to leave and started to conduct Geo's Ping-tung (city of south Taiwan close to the larger city Kaohsiung) branch.

After managing the Ping-tung branch for many years, Fu took over the Feng-shan and Dung-gang (cities close to Ping-tung) branches as his brothers had not managed them well. By accumulating much managerial experience, Fu wanted to set up his own clinic. Therefore, he established his own clinic in Zuo-ying district of Kaohsiung City. As the clinic went well, he later set up other clinics in Kaohsiung and Ping-tung successfully. Furthermore, under the influence of Geo, who had studied in the EMBA program at National Singapore University in 2001, Fu joined the EMBA program at National Sun Yat-sen University in 2004.

In 2006, Dr. Fu established The "X Chinese Medical Service Network". By this network, Dr. Fu integrated all his clinics to provide a comprehensive service for patients. Now the headquarters of X Chinese Medical Service Network is located at the Ping-tung main clinic, which consists of 8 branches and two hundred staff. The total capital is approximately NT$1.5 hundred million and annual sales is approximately NT$2.98 hundred million. Geo on the other hand has now started a chain of Chinese Medical Clinics on a franchising basis in Singapore.

3.2   *Data collection and analysis*

Within the EMBA program story-making and storytelling was used as a learning methodology. Thus the three stories in this chapter are built upon stories originally created by Dr. Fu. These original stories have then been processed in several stages involving the authors of this chapter. Thus they have successively been theorized and related to entrepreneurship theories. Methodologically therefore this chapter offers a quite unique approach to the development of a research text, which is produced within a dialogue between practitioner and researchers (Clandinin and Connelly, 2000).

Dr. Fu was one of the first author's students. When Fu began to ponder on the topic of his Masters thesis, the first author of this study encouraged him to write his own experience of managing Chinese medical clinics. Therefore, Fu narrated the story of his entrepreneurial process by himself and rebuilt the structure of each event with supervision from the first and third author. During this period, we had nine discussions, each lasting two hours. Aside from rebuilding the structure of each event, we also made clear the background and context in many events. Finally, Fu finished his thesis "The Research of Innovative Business Model in X Chinese Medical Clinic".

Therefore, the data collection and analysis in this study had two main stages: (1) from narrative materials to field texts and (2) from field texts to research texts. The first stage involved the cooperation between narrator and researcher. The narrator tape-recorded his own experience and discussed with the researchers to develop systematic stories as field texts. In the second stage, the researcher began to search for theory to interpret the field texts. We destructed and recombined the stories through theoretical perspectives and configured several story lines as research texts.

3.3 *From narrative materials to field texts*

Narrative material is fundamental to narrative research, which includes self-narration, real-life events, dialogues, conversations, and stories gained from interviews, etc. (Lieblich *et al.*, 1998; Clandinin and Connelly, 2000). Briefly speaking, narrative material is made up by written or spoken life experience in storied forms by narrators. Dr. Fu used tape-recording to narrate his life experience, which is the fundamental form of specific experiences in a narrator's real life (Riessman, 1993). The tapes equated the narrative material in its original appearance. This material needed to be sorted out systematically to produce field texts. Usually the tape-recording is done by the researcher, but here it was done by the narrator himself.

Field texts are most often produced by the researcher after transcribing the narrative materials. In this case, the researchers and the narrator cooperated in this process, the researcher as advisor to the narrator how to figure out a complete and systematic structure (Clandinin and Connelly, 2000). This procedure functioned to encourage more detailed background and context accounts so that new stories could be created. New narrative materials were thus added to produce new plot lines and to reconstruct original stories.

In our study, the basic narrative materials were stories narrated by Fu. The first author asked Fu to think about the most memorable experience in his managerial experience. Fu listed some events such as the reflections of managing the clinic, the experience of creating a new venture, his thoughts on Chinese medical science, and what he had learned through the EMBA program.

Because the first author felt that Fu's story was valuable for learning, he wanted Fu to narrate his experiences. As a result, Dr. Fu tape-recorded his own experience and asked his assistant to make transcriptions. In this process, Fu had recorded 600 minutes of oral storytelling, which amounted to 100 pages of transcripts.

There were several discussions between Fu and the researchers. Since most of the episodes in Fu's narrations were fragmentary narrated (see Table 1), Fu was asked to rearrange the transcripts based on the sequence of events narrated. During the process of transforming narrative materials to field texts, 33 events were categorized into six temporal stages based upon the dialogue between the narrator and the researchers (see Table 2).

Table 1.   Examples of transcribed text.

No.	Transcription
01	It was an amazing experience to start Yi Fan four years ago.
02	About four years ago, I was discussing with my two younger brothers at that time and during the conversation I became interested in opening a new clinic of my own.
03	That period of time was rather difficult for me because I was busy with matters in the Ping-tung clinic and the union at the same time. However, I have already come to a point of no return, so I had to think of some solutions.
04	As the idea is shaped out, I communicated with local administrative officers, and told them that I am willing to provide free medical checkup services in local veteran communities.
05	The plan to proceed was made up and there were twenty free medical checkup services, with each service lasting three to four days on one site. However, many obstacles emerged while we put our plan into practice, including lack of doctors and massagers and the hot weather. In order to cope with them, I made few rearrangements.
06	First, I rescheduled the doctors' sheets in the three existing clinics, and recruited and train new massagers. Then I coordinated the administrative staffs to support the free medical services.

For example, when Fu narrated why he used different managerial ways in different regions, he did not give the details. Through mutual dialogue, Fu added additional remarks such as the way how he observed and what he found concerning Feng-shan and Dong-gang branches have different population structures. In this process, the researchers could obtain a better understanding through the co-constructing and re-combining the raw material based upon ongoing conversations. For Fu, it was a learning experience to re-combine and re-construct his original narrative materials. As a result, the field texts were a joint effort (*cf.* Clandinin and Connelly, 2003).

3.4   *From field texts to research texts*

What was originally tape-recorded oral story-telling by Dr. Fu ended in mutually produced field texts categorized into temporal stages and narrated

Table 2. Categorization of stories.

Temporal stages	Events and examples
Family background	Story of grandfather, father's conservation, interactions among brothers, learning in China Medical University, my internship.
Experiences in being a Chinese medical doctor	First impression of being a doctor, how I interact with patients, family and medical meeting at the same time.
Experiences in taking over branches	Management in Ping-tung branch, doing a favor to my brothers, taking over Dong-gang branch, taking over Feng-shan branch.
Experiences in the establishment of Yi Fan	The reason to initiate my own clinic, picking up the location to establish the clinic, free medical treatment, Successive process in building up Yi Fan.
EMBA study	EMBA learning experience of third younger brother, my EMBA experiences.
Establishment of X Chinese Medical Clinic Alliance	Establishment of Ming Hou, ranking competition among Chinese medical doctors, SOP establishment.

events. From this point, the researcher reconstructed the field text into this research text. This process, first of all, was driven by the purpose to make a contribution to bring entrepreneurship and innovation together in the context of daily life experiences of the "entrepreneur".

Clandinin and Connelly (2003) have mentioned three necessary considerations in the methodology of narrative inquiry, which guided our process: consideration of theory, consideration of field text orientation, and consideration of interpretation and analysis. In consideration of theory, we explored our phenomenon by finding out the narrative perspective of the field texts. In consideration of field text orientation, we avoided contact and conversation with the narrator and concentrated on reading field texts to construct the research texts. In consideration of interpretation and analysis, we reflected about the relationship between field texts and research texts. We sought to find out what themes were "hidden" in the field texts, bearing in mind that the research texts first of all reflects how we, as researchers, experience the themes, not necessarily the same themes that would stand out for our narrator.

Based on these considerations, we have discussed, read, and self-enquired continuously while writing the research texts. The process of transforming field texts to research texts was as follows:

Stage 1: Early exploration on theoretical perspective

The third and fourth authors focused on the field texts individually to discover meaningful sections. A week after the discussion, we found that we mainly emphasized the transition of the narrator's roles. Therefore, we decided to focus on roles. We constructed a plot of "Chinese medical doctor, clinic director, and entrepreneur" to rewrite the stories collected in the final field texts.

But when we were ready to write the research texts, we faced the first problem, which was the theoretical perspective we applied. At this time, the most important step is to read some works by thoughtful researchers and authors (Clandinin and Connelly, 2003). Since we focused on the transition of the narrator's different roles, the search for related works or studies was our next goal. And then we defined three key words including "self, role, and transition" to help us search for reading materials. In later discussion, we found that *Modernity and Self-Identity* (Giddens, 1991) was on our booklists. This urged us to connect the transition of narrator's roles with identity. For that reason, we reconstructed the meaning of the original field texts based on the theory of identity.

Stage 2: The writing and transference from interim texts

When we interpreted the meaning of original field texts from the perspective of identity, we constructed the following three themes; "the construct and display of professional identity", "the construct and display of managerial identity", and "the construct and display of entrepreneurial identity". According to these themes, we rewrote the plots and episodes in each theme to produce the first version of research text. However, when rethinking our research issue on entrepreneurship, we faced our first frustration in interpretation and analysis. We realized a connection between entrepreneurship and identity but we were not satisfied about how we interpreted this relationship.

Therefore, we began to hold two one-hour discussions every week to analyze the details in each plot. After three months of discussion, we noted several key events, including Fu becoming a chief upon his brother's request and learning to be a manager through facing real problems. Moreover, the experience of managing the clinic stimulated Fu to establish his own clinic and transformed him to an entrepreneur. In this transition, Fu's self-identity has transformed as well. On one hand, Fu still kept his original self-identity. On the other hand, Fu shaped a new identity. We discovered the theme of multi-identity in this process and rewrote the second research text that include three themes of "the construct and display of identity", "the overlap of multi-identity", and "the leap of multi-identity".

Stage 3: The re-exploration of theoretical perspective

By way of the first stages, we interpreted different meanings through the perspective of identity. We realized identity attached to different roles and the intertwined relationship between identities in the first and second interim texts. However, this did not explain our research interest in entrepreneurship and innovative behaviors. We thought that there may be some invisible connections in the field texts that we have not discussed yet.

As a result, we read and discussed extensively to identify any new developments since there might be some profound meanings that we had not perceived in the narrative stories. In this stage, we defined "entrepreneurship" as the keyword and tried to review the related literature. Based on the studies of Rae and Carswell (2001) and Johansson (2004), we gained some insights on "identity", "entrepreneur's learning", "practical theory", and "imitative innovation", etc.

We then recombined and analyzed the stories and found several important constructs such as identity, problem, narrative knowing, and self-interpretation. Next, we paid close attention to each plot and held three one-hour discussions every week. After three months, we realized that Fu displays entrepreneurship and innovation in his daily practice. Finally, we focused on the themes of practice and entrepreneurship. And based on "practice theoretical perspective", we recombined the whole story's plots as our third version of research texts.

4　Story and Analysis

4.1　*The emergence of managerial sense*

Life narratives intertwine personal actions and historical context (Elder and Shananan, 1997). Fu's stories illustrate similar construction process, although being even more complex as is also intertwined with the context of the researchers and their theoretical interpretative repertoire. In this section, we present the stories that capture the process of the way Dr. Fu transited from a professional doctor to a Chinese clinic director in the Ping-tung branch. The insight is depicted from the hidden scene concerning how his attitude was transformed from passive to more aggressive when facing various and complex managerial works in the process.

When Fu had graduated from China Medical University, he worked for his father's clinic. As a professional doctor, he spent much time to diagnose his patients during the daytime and enjoyed reading books related to medicine to enhance his knowledge in his leisure time. When Fu's brother requested his help to be the director of Ping-tung branch, Fu faced a dilemma.

> Well, I faced a difficult situation... move to Ping-tung or stay here... tell the truth, on one hand I was afraid to leave my home that I was used to, on the other hand, I felt that maybe I could do something different in Ping-tung branch.

People tend to feel a sense of security in familiar places; on the other hand, they look for variation in daily routine life. Fu had an inner desire to move on and at the same time had feelings of uncertainty toward his situation. Fu had to face some critical choices in order to step forward. In situations like this, people need some self-reflection between disparities of comfort zone and unfamiliarity to make their own decisions (Giddens, 1991). Finally, Fu decided to give himself a chance to move forward in continuing a self-reflective process.

During the first month, Fu became uncomfortable with his work. He regarded himself as a Chinese medical doctor. His mission, as a professional in Chinese medicine was to treat patients. Dealing and helping patients was his love and passion. At this moment, Fu, however, became overwhelmed by daily routines and dragged by those miscellaneous issues (e.g., patients' complaints, senatorial works, administrative bureaucracies), as he had became the Director of Ping-tung clinic. With deep frustration, Fu questioned his own decision.

> Before I went to Ping-tung, I had much time to treat patients and also had some free time for myself... but now, I have lots of meetings... I had a difficulty sleeping at night... I regret I made this decision. There are many problems in my life.

From the above quotes, we can see the nonequilibrium of Fu's mood. In this condition, people need some time to reconstruct their inner psychological conditions. Fu sometimes chose to be alone and went away from his troublesome and messy working environment to a coffee shop. One day, he went to a coffee shop and took his seat. After a while, he overheard a comment from the coffee shop owner to his manager. "What an administrator should care about is the whole process of operation, not only the tiny details". This sentence was just like a key to trigger Fu's mind to remind him that he is also a manager in addition to his profession.

During the psychological reconstructing process of an individual, any tiny action or a passing conversation could be a trigger to make an impact on inner world reconstruction (Giddens, 1991). Fu was inspired by overhearing this specific conversation, his heart was struck at that moment. An idea emerged that "if I am a director, I should take care of the whole operation rather than the tiny details on clinic business". said Fu.

Fu began to negotiate with himself what his role and responsibilities as a manager should be. Such self-reflection and self-reconstruction process mirrors "the emergence of a specific managerial sense". A managerial sense is not there from the start as soon as the manager role begins. It emerges partly due to inner reflections and outer contextual engagements.

As this story goes, when Fu realized what a manager should do, he began to try and to find some ways in dealing with clinic administrative works. In the meantime, he related to insightful incidents emerging from the Chinese herbal medicine course which he attended in medical college.

> Chinese herbal medicine is very complicated... the doctor must identify the exact and appropriate medicine for the right patient... While I was studying Chinese pharmacology, I found that there are certain elements which could be categorized... I sorted out the herbal medicine accordingly. In this way, it helps me to memorize those intricate nuances and my Chinese pharmacology grades were outstanding.

Fu recalled the class he took at China Medical University. There are numerous Chinese herbals for treatment of various diseases. In this class he was able to improvise the most effective way of memorization and classification of herbal medicine. Fu thought perhaps the various and complex managerial works are similar to the intricate relations that Chinese herbal medicine has encompassed that he had experienced in the Chinese medicine course. And then he tried to figure that out following the logic he employed to arrange his herbal medicine study. "I tried to classify the issues which are proposed in the meeting next morning and found that there are some patterns..."

said Fu. This process of learning and applying herbs for treatment intrigues Fu to pay more attention to the main points of management.

Hence, we find Fu through recalling his experience of learning Chinese herbal medicine and tried to prioritize clinical affairs and classify them into different hierarchical categories and assign them to employees who should carry out the tasks. This process that Fu has demonstrated is what Bruner (1986) proposed as "narrative knowing". Fu found different ways about his managerial works from his personal real life experiences and stories that had significant meanings and provided contextual and spatial thinking, therefore he gained some clues from narrative structure and identified the ways to deal with his problems.

In concluding this part of the story, we can realize how Fu's managerial sense emerged in his narrations. Fu's self-managerial sense originated from interaction with social contexts which he faced. Through this emergence of self-managerial sense, Fu faced the complex clinic administrative works aggressively. In addition to his new aggressiveness toward his administrative activities, he also applied the learning experience of herbal medicine to deal with the complex clinical affairs. He knew he had to prioritize and make systematic arrangements about how to conduct clinical works in this process.

4.2   *Forming and utilizing personal theory from practice*

People refer to their past experiences which they use to meet and figure out the framework of problem solutions when faced with the unknown and uncertain situations (Giddens, 1991). In this section, we focus on Fu's life narration reflecting how he took over Dong-gang branch and Feng-shan branch. We want to illustrate what problems Fu faced in these new branches and how Fu overcame the problems he faced during this period.

Fu continued to be in charge of Ping-tung branch, and he made it performed much better when it compared to the time Geo was in charge. Geo took into account Fu's good performance as well as his own plan to open a new branch in Singapore. Therefore, Geo anticipated that Fu could take over his Dong-gang branch. Due to Fu's successful experience on Ping-tung clinic, he was willing to be the director of a new branch. So Fu accepted his brother's request determinedly. But when Fu came to Dong-gang branch in the first month, he realized there were many unexpected challenges to enhance administrative efficiency and the number of patients.

> When I went to Dong-gang branch, I noticed inefficiency in administrative works and also lack of sufficient patients... the total income was not enough to cover the whole operational cost...

In this situation, Fu referred to his past experiences in Ping-tung branch to offer some promotions such as free registration fee and provided some free ointments to the patients. The result of those measures increased the number of patients and improved the financial condition in Dong-gang branch. After a few months, Fu's forth brother also observed the well performance from Fu's management. Therefore, he requested Fu to take over his Feng-shan branch. Fu was willing to take this offer and speculated he is able to handle Feng-shan branch based on his successful experiences from previous cases.

When Fu went to Feng-shan branch, he noticed the similar problems concerning administrative inefficiency and lack of sufficient patients for business. Fu followed the same logical line of thought and employed the similar skills to solve problems at this new branch. But the result was beyond his expectation. The successful operation system in Dong-gang branch had failed in the new Feng-shan branch. This situation confused Fu.

> I used the same ways to improve the Feng-shan branch, but it does not work as better as Dong-gang branch did. I didn't know what goes wrong in this condition.

In order to understand what went wrong, Fu decided to conduct field observation to find out why different results come out when he conducted the same way of operations. *"I went around and interviewed local people surrounding Feng-shan branch. I tried to find out the causality to such unexpected results."* From this remark, we can tell Fu has begun to shape new way out in dealing his business problem. He conducted field observations to learn the reason why his successful model is inapplicable in his new branch.

> I found there was something different in those places; I felt the residents had more close ties and connection in Ping-tung and Dong-gang, they always communicated with each other frequently... but this was not the same in Feng-shan... I felt residents didn't interact as frequently in Feng-shan... Therefore, I think that Ping-tung and Dong-gang belong to more close community ties, where as Feng-shan belongs to a more open community...

Fu made conclusions based upon field observations as well as previous experience and then formed his personal theory to explain what situation he met. Fu could engage residents by word-of-mouth in close communities because of close ties in Ping-tung and Dong-gang, but maybe he needed other ways to face the residents in Feng-shan branch. From his observation, this area draws a lot of immigrants from adjoining cities to Feng-shan and most of them are young people working in high-tech or international trade companies. They are unfamiliar with one another. Thus there is less interactions between them. These people are educated in the western system, which makes them more newfangled and they are likely to challenge the traditional medicine. Fu began to introduce some instruments from western medicine in order to attract and engage residents in Feng-shan branch (e.g. infrared rays to treat muscular problems and relieve pain).

After almost two months, Fu was able to increase the number of patients in Feng-shan branch. From the story, we can tell entrepreneurial learning is related to the process of interaction between individual and social context (Minniti and Bygrave, 2001). From a contextual-social interaction perspective, the entrepreneur's inner mindset framework, by learning from past experiences, will change and transform as it engaged in upcoming different situations.

The following case makes this argument more apparently. Although Fu had formed his personal theory about how to operate the clinics in different areas, he still encountered great difficulties in Zuo-ying branch. Zuo-ying is in the border area in business center of Kaohsiung city where many military camps are set up. Therefore, the residents mostly were soldiers and their families. Fu faced a very different situation in Zuo-ying, he employed free diagnosis and treatment to promote his clinic and to gather the information concerning patients' needs initially. Indeed Fu's business story illustrates how people create meaning and action through personal theory (Shotter, 1995).

In concluding this part of the story, we realized how Fu formed and utilized personal theory to solve problems by his narration. As Maturana and Varela(1998) argued: "Every action is knowing and every knowing is action." Furthermore, through Fu's narration we saw the process of how he put his knowing into action. Fu used his stories to conduct his daily practice, reflected upon them, came up with solutions through continuous exploration and adaptation, and then accumulated his personal theory. The life story perspective adopted here illustrates how such business know-how is created. It is in the story that a sequence of events and incidents take place and delicate nuances which treated as a black box in previous entrepreneurship literatures was articulated, and the meaningful insights were depicted from it.

4.3 The re-interpreting of "imitation to creation"

Ricoeur (1984) has argued that it would shape out various frameworks for an individual to recognize the world when he or she has conducted different social interactions as well as experienced various contexts. As a result, multiple and fruitful circumstances can be taken as a useful resource to facilitate individuals building up their mindset. Bear this theoretical concern in mind, Fu's narrative regarding his EMBA experience intrigues our attention.

With the encouragement from Geo, Fu started EMBA program in 2004. Fu's classmates in the EMBA program came from diverse business fields, and they were quite experienced in their business. Fu mentioned that he was able to observe their distinguished practices and gained various stimulations through interactions with classmates when he engaged in EMBA program. He told a story about the "Class Regulation Proposal Contest" which prompted him to relate to the establishment of SOPs for his clinic.

Fu recalled from his memory in the beginning of a specific school day. His classmates regarded the class rules is necessary for guiding and running class matters, they wanted to discuss how to make these rules. Ted who is a high-tech engineer and considered as a brilliant guy had proposed a "Class Regulation Proposal Contest" to the public, when most of students had remained silent. The Class Regulation Proposal Contest required every classmate to deliver their ideas regarding "what as well as how" the class should be regulated. Then the best proposal was selected among submissions by the whole members in the class meeting. The silence was broke by Ted's idea, and everyone seemed to be motivated and started to think how to propose ideas. It shaped out a platform for classmates to facilitate dialogue and communicate ideas. And the competition mechanism provides a mean for those classmates who were either managers or CEOs to prove themselves as the winner. As a result, the "Class Regulation Proposal Contest" turned out a functional outcome that facilitated the process and came up with a comprehensive regulation. This process had inspired Fu. He pondered over if he could relate this event to the management of his Chinese medical clinics.

Through the process of Class Regulation Proposal Contest, some meaningful observations had made by Fu. Firstly, the profile of EMBA classmates is quite similar with his clinics' staffs (e.g. administrative, nurses and therapists), as they are autonomous professionals and not easy to be motivated. Secondly, Class Regulation Proposal Contest provides a good motivation mechanism for his classmates and Fu thought this probably could be useful to prompt his staffs as well. So Fu started to think how he could apply this model to establish SOPs for his clinic alliance.

> Ah..m, I think the class rule is a good mean to make efficient coordination for classmates. And it makes me start to think ... if I could proceed and organize my clinics like this way.

Practical action can be an analytic instrument for actors to identify and recognize the connections between practice and living as well as create meanings from it (Shotter, 1993, 1995). For Fu, his observation of Class Regulation Proposal Contest took shape as a medium by which he could find some hints and start to relate some critical elements to the establishment of SOPs in Chinese clinics. In the first place he simply tried to imitate the idea of Class Regulation Proposal Contest and proceed to the "SOPs Proposal Contest" in his clinics.

First, Fu classified his employees according to their different professions into three categories — Nursing, Therapy and Administration. Then Fu asked staffs to deliver their ideas of SOP corresponding with their profession to the committee. Then the clinic committee will sort out the best ones as SOPs in their clinic alliance. It turned out, however, failure when this model was tested. Only three proposals were received one month later.

Fu elaborately pondered over why it turned out in this way. Apparently, it worked in the EMBA setting. Why could it not work out as it did in his clinic? The reason Fu found why it works in EMBA was because his classmates wanted to say something but they lacked the appropriate context to deliver their ideas. Since everyone has high social esteem and they do not like to break their friendship initially as their inappropriate ideas could be offensive. Under such circumstance, the Class Regulation Proposal Contest provided a platform for them to share ideas.

On the contrary, employees in the clinic do not have such initiatives. Thus it failed when the concept was imitated exactly. Furthermore, Fu made a modification by adding incentives into the SOP Proposal Contest. First, he gave $500 to those who deliver their proposals. Second, the winner will receive $50,000 plus three day off as a reward. And most of all, the winner will be promoted as an SOP leader in teaching other clinic staffs how to proceed the SOPs. By such amendment, the SOPs came out and established in the divisions of Nursing and Administration. It did not work out, however, in division of Therapy. Therapists conveyed their vulnerability in conducting SOPs in this way. Since their operations are hardly to put into text, they have to demonstrate with their practices. As this consideration, Fu made an adjustment for Therapy by adding the demonstration contest. All therapists in the clinic alliance were gathered in the headquarter and demonstrated their therapy to compete their ideal SOPs. Then the best demonstration was selected by the committee, and came out as the ideal SOPs for the division of Massage therapy.

The above story has explained how Fu related the idea of Class Regulation Proposal Contest to the application of clinics SOPs establishment. As a result, Fu's imitation contributes to creation. Johansson (2007) has deconstructed the ideas of imitation and creation in the entrepreneurial research. He has suggested that individual can imitate what he is good at and create something new from it.

From the Fu's story we can see imitation of other's practice. Fu tried to copy what his classmate's demonstration to SOPs establishment. Although, the initial hard copy did not work out a good result while Fu applied it to his clinics. However, he added his contextual amendments to make it work. From this process, Fu implemented "imitation to creation" with his reinterpretation of classmate's practice. Initially, Fu detected that the motivation mechanism of Class Regulation Proposal Contest did not work to encourage his employees. From his understanding and comparison, he figured out the problem was the lack of tangible incentives for clinics' staffs. Furthermore, the therapists' vulnerability to conduct SOPs in paper work is comprehended by Fu as he is sophisticated in how massage therapy service is provided. Then he made another amendment for the division of Therapists.

In concluding this part of the story, we highlight two critical findings which could deepen what Johansson(2007) has argued: (1) Other's practice can be a good medium for "imitation to creation", as we can tell from the story; the "Class Regulation Proposal Contest" shapes out a template for Fu to ponder over how he can proceed to SOPs establishment, (2) Situated interpretation is a key to make this "imitation to creation" possible: Fu has put the contextual knowing which gathered from his experience in Chinese medical clinic to re-interpret the Class Regulation Proposal Contest, then he made the appropriate amendments which correspond to the situated context and establish SOPs successfully.

5   Conclusion and Implication

Traditionally, the topic of family business is discussed through the economic perspective and that the "agent problem" is one of major issues. The management and ownership are discussed and contribute lots of resources to ease or align the asymmetry between business owners and professional managers. However, it is so limited while the lens we apply only from the economic aspect.

The economic idea considers the objective in question piece by piece in order to analyze it easily. However, it narrows the scope and hampers the other possibilities. Within the traditional discussion in family business, the environment, actions, and individuals are independent elements, and the environment is considered as a constraint to individuals, and leads a given hypothesis that individual is "bounded rationality". Due to this assumption, there are many discussions in family business studies on how to delegate business administration to a professional manager. Hence, the information asymmetry among managers and owners are highlighted. In Fu's story, we try to shift from economics view to social constructionism ideas.

It is, however, not the same discussion while we shift to the more dynamic idea which social constructionism addressed. As Giddens mentioned the interrelationship between structure and actor, between duality of structure provided and agency which actor possesses in his structuration theory (Giddens, 1994). This idea can shed a light on how we can release the discussions about "management vs. ownership", "insider (heir) vs. outsider (professional manager)" and old vs. new" etc., in existing family business.

In Fu's story, he demonstrated how he embedded himself into Chinese medicine and employed his agency to interact with constraints and enabling that provided by defaulted setting in the clinics that belonged to his brothers. And those innovative management and business conducting are crafted from the interrelated interactions between Fu and structures (clinics, different markets, different settings such as EMBA).

Through the inspiration of social constructionism, we study Fu's everyday life and every stage of practice and reflexivity. Some fresh ideas are bubbled to the surface. Family business is not the static objective for being given or inherited. It presents a different kind of platform to stimulate entrepreneurial spirits in Fu's family. Chinese medicine is the medium that connected Fu's father and his brothers. And the point of traditional business mind collides with novel business ideas. Then the conflict paved a way for Fu to start his journey as an entrepreneur. And we learned from Fu's story, entrepreneurship is the accumulative result of an individual's daily interactions. Fu's entrepreneurship process from being a professional doctor to additionally assuming the role of a manager and entrepreneur enabled us to have a better understanding of entrepreneurship.

First, "identity" motivates entrepreneurship. In the process of Fu's managing clinical problems, we observed that Fu overcame his self-consciousness while facing his problems. Under Fu's managerial identity, he was willing to confront his own problems and searched for solutions. Therefore, identity becomes a motivation that shapes entrepreneurship.

Second, "personal theory" is fundamental in pursuing entrepreneurship. Fu developed his own business theory from his managerial experiences in Feng-shan and Dong-gang branches, such as the perceptions of "open community" and "closed community". The personal theory that Fu has formed through the process of practice becomes the foundation for a business creation.

Third, it is important to reinforce entrepreneurship with field training. Although Fu formulated personal theory by past experiences, the innovative effect is limited. Such application is confined to medical service business and limited creations could come out. When Fu engaged in the EMBA program, he faced new environments, which provide abundant stimulus that contributes to his advanced innovation. For example, through Class Regulation Proposal Contest, Fu came up with various ways to run his clinic. As we can note, in this process, Fu was not merely a copycat but made reinterpretations according to the situations at the clinic. Hence, new field practices are fruitful source to reinforce and escalate an individual's entrepreneurship.

From these discussions, we have realized some of the implications of how to engage in entrepreneurial behaviors in a sequential process. First, we ought to emphasize the shaping of an entrepreneur's identity through encouraging an individual to confront his problems. Encouraging one to tackle with problems is the key to construct self-consciousness and identity. Moreover, we ought to develop a personal theory through open learning instead of simply following principles. This will enable an individual to learn from his problem-solving process, develop the ability of sense-making, and eventually shape his entrepreneurship. Finally, we ought to encourage an entrepreneur to explore and practice instead of mere control. By doing so, an individual could have various daily interactions in different settings which would strengthen his entrepreneurship.

Theoretically, the stories contribute to a narrative approach to entrepreneurship. It builds upon but goes further than previous studies that have used the stories of entrepreneurs' to understand their learning process (Rae, 2004; Johansson, 2004). Furthermore, the stories contribute to the understanding of innovation and creativity as the core of entrepreneurship. As well, they provide an interesting case of family succession, where contradictions lead to further innovation. A family heritage is transformed into something quite new. As a whole, the chapter responds to the call for process studies in the field of entrepreneurship (Gartner, 1985; Gartner and Brush, 2007; Steyaert, 2007; Ucbasaran *et al.*, 2001).

References

Bertaux, D. and M. Kohli (1984). The life story approach: A continental view, *Annual Review of Sociology*, 10, 215–237.

Bruner, J. (1986). *Actual Minds, Possible Worlds*, Cambridge, MA: Harvard University Press.

Bruner, J. (1990). *Acts of Meaning*, MA: Harvard University Press.

Casillas, J. and F. Acedo (2007). Evolution of the intellectual structure of family business literature: A bibliometric study of FBR, *Family Business Review*, 20(2), 141–162.

Chamberlayne, P., J. Bornat, T. Wengraf (eds.) (2000). *The Turn to Biographical Methods in Social Science Comparative Issues and Examples*, New York: Routledge.

Clandinin, D. J. and F. M. Connelly (2000). *Narrative Inquiry: Experience and Story in Qualitative Research*, San Francisco, CA: Jossey-Bass.

Cunningham, J. B. and J. Lischeron (1991). Defining entrepreneurship, *Journal of Small Business Management*, 29, 45–61.

Drucker, P. (1985). *Innovation and Entrepreneurship*, New York: Harper and Row.

Elder, H. G. and M. J. Shananan (1997). Nested Comparisons in the Study of Human Development: Linking Social Change and Individual Adaptation, in J. Tudge, M. J. Shanahan, and J. Valsiner (eds.), *Comparisons in Human Development: Understanding Time and Context*, New York: Cambridge University Press, 109–136.

Gartner, W. B. (1985). *Entrepreneurs and Entrepreneurship: Process Versus Content Approaches*, Unpublished Manuscript, Georgetown University.

Gartner, W. B. and C. B. Brush (2007). *Entrepreneurship as Organizing: Emergence, Newness and Transformation*, in T. Habbershop, and

M. Rice (eds.), Praeger Perspectives on Entrepreneurship, 1–20, CT: Praeger Publishers.

Giddens, A. (1991). *Modernity and Self-Identity*, Cambridge: Polity Press.

Giddens, A. (1984). The Constitution of Society: outline of the theory of structuration. Berkeley, CA: University of California Press.

Johansson, A. W. (2004). Narrating the entrepreneur, *International Small Business Journal*, 22(3), 273–293.

Johansson, A. W. (2006). Mediating between creativity and innovation in entrepreneurship theory. Presented at the 14th Nordic Conference on Small Business Research in Stockholm, 11th–13th May 2006.

Knight, F. (1921). *Risk, Uncertainty, and Profit*, Boston: Houghton Mifflin.

Lave, J. (1988). *Cognition in Practice*, UK: Cambridge University Press.

Lieblich, A., R. Tuval-Mashiach and T. Zilber (1998). *Narrative Research: Reading, Analysis and Interpretation*, Thousand Oaks, CA: Sage.

Low, M. B. and I. C. MacMillan (1988). Entrepreneurship: Past research and future challenges, *Journal of Management*, 14(2), 139–161.

Maturana, H. R. and F. J. Varela (1998). *The Three of Knowledge: The Biological Roots of Human Understanding*, Boston: Shambhala Publications.

Minniti, M. and W. D. Bygrave (2001). A dynamic model of entrepreneurial learning, *Entrepreneurship Theory and Practice*, 25, 5–16.

Morck, R. K. and L. Steier (2005). The global history of corporate governance — An introduction, Chicago: University of Chicago Press.

Orlikowski, W. J. (2002). Knowing practice: Enacting a collective capability in distributed organizing, *Organization Science*, 13(3), 249–273.

Pitt, M. (1998). A tale of two gladiators: 'Reading' entrepreneurs as texts, *Organization Studies*, 19(3): 387–414.

Rae, D. and M. Carswell (2001). Towards a conceptual understanding of entrepreneurial learning, *Journal of Small Business & Enterprise Development*, 8(2), 150–158.

Rae, D. (2004). Practical theories from entrepreneurs' stories: discursive approaches to entrepreneurial learning, *Journal of Small Business and Enterprise Development*, 11(2): 195–202.

Rae, D. and M. Carswell (2000). Using a life-story approach in researching entrepreneurial learning: The development of a conceptual model and its implications in the design of learning experiences, *Education & Training*, 42(4), 220–227.

Riessman, C. K. (1993). *Narrative Analysis*, Newbury Park: SAGE.

Ricoeur, P. (1984). *Time and Narrative*, Vol 1., Chicago: The University of Chicago Press.

Schön, D. A. (1983). *The Reflective Practitioner*, New York: Basic Books.

Schumpeter, J. A. (1934). *The Theory of Economic Development*, Cambridge, MA: Harvard University Press.

Shane, S. and S. Venkataraman (2000). The promise of entrepreneurship as a field of research, *Academy of Management Review*, 25(1), 217–226.

Sharma, P. (2004). An overview of the field of family business studies: Current status and directions for the future, *Family Business Review*, 27(1), 1–36.

Shotter, J. (1993). *Conversational Realities: Constructing Life Through Language*. Thousand Oak, CA: Sage.

Shotter, J. (1995), The manager as a practical author: A rhetorical-responsive, social constructionist approach to social-organizational problems, in D-M. Hosking, H. P. Dachler, and K. J. Gergen (eds.), *Management and Organisation: Relational Alternatives to Individualism*, Avebury: Aldershot, 99–117.

Smart, J. (1994). Business Immigration to Canada: Deception and Exploitation: In *Reluctant Exiles? Migration from Hong Kong and the New Overseas Chinese*, Ronald Skeldon (ed.), Armonk, New York: M.E. Sharpe, 98–119.

Steyaert, C. (2004). *The Prosaics of Entrepreneurship*, in D. Hjorth and C. Steyaert (eds.), *Narrative and Discursive Approaches in Entrepreneurship*, Cheltenham: Edward Elgar, 8–21.

Steyaert, C. (2007). Entrepreneuring as a conceptual attractor? A review of process theories in 20 years of entrepreneurship studies, *Entrepreneurship & Regional Development*, 19(11), 453–477.

Ucbasaran, D., P. Westhead and M. Wright (2001). The focus of entrepreneurial research: Contextual and process issues, *Entrepreneurship: Theory and Practice*, 25, 57–80.

Yamada, J. I. (2004). A multi-dimensional view of entrepreneurship — Toward a research agenda on organization emergence, *Journal of Management Development*, 23(4), 289–320.

PART 2

Advanced Service Management in the Public and Non-Profit Organizations

7
Performance Management Systems of Japanese Local Governments

Takami Matsuo
Kobe University

1 Introduction

From the latter half of the 1990s, the management environment surrounding local governments in Japan changed significantly. As the tax revenue growth rate declined from the 1990s onward, administrative demand, such as public investment and social welfare programs, continued to grow, so the financial condition of many local governments deteriorated. As a result, even Japan, which had been conservative toward New Public Management (NPM) in OECD countries, decided to implement NPM from the end of the 1990s.

The approach in Japan is characterized primarily by Policy, Program and Project-based evaluation (PPP evaluation), which many local governments have practiced since 2000. This has played a certain role in securing accountability to citizens, but in terms of management decision-making, such as planning and budget preparation, many local governments have faced challenges. During these approximately 10 years, local governments have searched for good practices toward improving the usefulness of evaluation data in decision-making by taking various approaches.

This article introduces the evaluation methods that local governments in Japan have implemented in order to increase the usefulness of evaluation data in decision-making. It divides evaluation methods into internal and external evaluations and absolute and relative evaluations. The characteristics and potential of each are studied.

2 Changes in the Management Environment around Local Governments and NPM

Since the 1980s, NPM has been pursued in the UK, New Zealand, and other Anglo-Saxon countries. Based on studies in the latter half of the 1990s, Guthrie *et al.* (1999) indicate that Japan is very conservative among OECD countries. However, at the time, Japan was beginning to focus on NPM, and the central government and some local governments were proceeding to study NPM.

First, in terms of the financial accounting system, in 2000 the Ministry of Internal Affairs and Communications presented a method of preparing balance sheets based on annual account settlement statistics. In 2001, standards for preparing administrative cost statements, and in 2006, standards for preparing balance sheets, administrative cost statements, cash flow statements, statements of changes in net assets, and consolidated financial statements were presented, so the concept of double-entry bookkeeping and accrual accounting was gradually introduced. In addition, in terms of the audit system, in 1999 a comprehensive external audit system was introduced, and external audits are becoming more rigorous.

In introducing market mechanisms, the designated manager system was adopted in 2003 so that the management and operation of public facilities could be consigned to private enterprises. In 2006, the Public Service Reform Act was enacted, which enabled public–private competitive bidding (market testing) and opened reception work and so forth to the private sector. PPP evaluation is a result-oriented performance management system, which has rapidly spread since 2000.

In terms of decentralization and the relationship between central government ministries/agencies and local governments, in 2000 the Law Concerning Preparations of Related Laws for the Promotion of Decentralization was enacted and tax revenues were shifted to the regional level, but this has not led to much change in the authority of local governments.

3 Approaches to and Challenges in Administrative Evaluation

Among NPM activities in Japanese local governments, PPP evaluation has had the most significant effect. PPP evaluation has the following characteristics:

(1) It is in line with hierarchical comprehensive planning structures such as Policy (e.g., improvement in the basic academic skills of elementary and middle school students), Program (e.g., spread of healthy eating habits), and Project (e.g., school meal service).
(2) Measure not only invested resources (input) for Programs and Projects but also output and outcomes, and evaluate these from multiple perspectives, such as economic viability, efficiency, effectiveness, and urgency.
(3) Management is oriented toward MBO (Management by Objectives). In addition, in the process of implementing PDCA cycles, communication within organizations is emphasized.
(4) Evaluation data is used in management for distributing resources (budgeting), forming plans, and so forth.
(5) Evaluation data is publicly disclosed to residents and contributes to the clarification of accountability.

This type of PPP evaluation was implemented in the latter half of the 1990s by some local governments, such as Mie Prefecture. Subsequently, the Ministry of Internal Affairs and Communications, the Board of Audit, the Cabinet Office, and other entities in the central government did not put in place a legal system, but the Ministry of Internal Affairs and Communications provided information to local governments throughout Japan, and the "Administrative Reform Guidelines" adopted by the Cabinet in 2000 clearly stated that administrative evaluation would be promoted, so implementation has progressed since 2000. Implementation is almost complete (more than 95% according to a study by the Ministry of Internal Affairs and Communications in 2010) in large localities, such as prefectures and government-designated cities, and even among all local governments, including cities, towns, and villages, more than 50% have already implemented program and project evaluation. The number of businesses to be evaluated, choice of evaluation criteria, measurement of outcomes, and evaluation methods in program and project evaluation were not mandated by the national government, but rather left up to the independent discretion of each local government. However, an evaluation system with the above-mentioned basic characteristics spread throughout Japan. In this sense, "institutional isomorphism", a concept developed by DiMaggio and Powell (1983), can be recognized.

PPP evaluation is a performance management system with a high degree of freedom and independence in terms of permitting each local government

Table 1.   Multi-factor evaluation in Yokohama city.

Category	Item
Relevance	Adaptability for social needs
	Necessity of government
Effectiveness	Validity of approach
	Degree of contribution to objectives
Level of achievement	Validity of target
	Target vs. result (output/outcome)
Efficiency	Cost reduction
	Productivity of business processing
Accuracy	Accuracy of business processing
	Accessibility of information

Source: Matsuo, 2009.

to establish evaluation system options and target values in line with their goals. For example, in Yokohama, the following multi-factor evaluation was implemented (Table 1).

Meanwhile, because the national government did not indicate any uniform evaluation criteria and standards, the comparability of evaluation data lowered. Quantitatively measuring the outcome of administrative activities is difficult to begin with (Lapsley, 1999; Kelly, 2002; Yamada, 2006), and it has also been indicated that establishing rational target values and rationally showing the relationship with input is difficult (e.g., Flynn, 1986, p. 397; Poister, 2003, p. 19; Osumi, 1999, pp. 55–56; Yamaguchi, 2008, p. 83). In Japan, comparability is poor, so it is more difficult to establish rational criteria options and targets, which was a major challenge in implementing administrative evaluation (e.g., Furukawa and Kitaoji, 2001; Yamamoto, 2001). According to research by Matsuo (2009) in 2008,[1] approximately 90% of companies implementing PPP evaluation have faced challenges in selecting evaluation criteria and establishing target values, and approximately 60% of local governments realize the difficulty of reflecting these in their budget-making. In addition, as shown in Fig. 1, in a study

---

[1]A fact-finding survey on the status of administrative evaluations of 853 local governments from November to December 2007. A total of 559 local governments (65.5%) responded, so there was no non-response bias.

done by the Ministry of Internal Affairs and Communication in October 2010, 79.1% of local governments recognize the establishment of evaluation criteria as a challenge, and 65% of local governments recognize their use in budget-making as a challenge (Ministry of Internal Affairs and Communication, 2010), with their usefulness in management decision-making for planning and budget preparation particularly low (Table 2).

4   How to Overcome the Challenges

There are many ways to increase the usefulness of evaluation data in decision-making in Japan (Matsuo, 2009), but provided that evaluations are done within an organization, they can be divided into four methods: increase the validity of evaluations through efforts within an organization, outsource evaluations, perform absolute evaluations, or perform relative evaluations.

First is to increase the accuracy of absolute evaluations within local governments, which is an approach for increasing objectivity, reliability, and validity through abundant data, multi-factor evaluation, and detailed evaluation criteria. Second is to try implementing relative evaluation within an organization. Each department ranks projects, and through discussions involving the mayor, officials, and department heads, overall rankings are decided. Third is the method of outsourcing evaluations. After evaluations are done within an organization, they are discussed in the assembly. Four is relative ranking.

In the following, based on a follow-up study by Matsuo (2009) and new case study research, the potential and challenges of each approach are examined. Internal/absolute evaluation is explained based on the author's previous research. Internal/relative evaluation is addressed in the case study of Yao City. Outsourcing/absolute evaluation is addressed in the case study of Itami City, and outsourcing/relative is based on documents and interviews.

5   Absolute Evaluation within the Organization

Independent approaches by local governments attempt to increase objectivity, reliability, and validity through abundant data, multi-factor evaluation, and detailed evaluation criteria. For example, Sendai City implemented a performance management system using an operational management chart in 2003. This classified more than 600 organizational challenges

Table 2. Difficulties in performance evaluation.

	Prefecture		Ordinance-designated (major) city		Heartland city		Specially-designated city		City and special ward		Town and village		Total	
	Number	%	Number	%	Number	%	Number	%	Number	%	Number	%	Number	%
Setting of relevant indicators	36	78.3	18	100	32	84.2	35	85.4	447	80.7	205	73.2	773	79.1
Feedback to the budgetary process	29	63	12	66.7	27	71.1	37	90.2	385	69.5	145	51.8	635	65.0
Population parameter (the number of implementation of performance evaluation)	46	100	18	100	38	100	41	100	554	100	280	100	977	100.0

Source: Ministry of Public Management, Home Affairs, Posts and Telecommunications, 2010.

(e.g., reduction of environmental load) into large categories (reduction in the final amount of disposed trash), medium categories (promotion of reuse as a resource), and small categories (separate collection of resource trash), and attempted to link this to improvements in business and operational procedures by further organizing the small categories by the amount of work and process. However, with approximately 13,000 at the small category level (2006), there were too many items to manage, and the effects did not match the cost of management, so in 2009 this system was stopped. Similarly, in 2001, Yokosuka City aimed to build a highly objective evaluation system through evaluations based on resident awareness survey data (e.g., level of importance, level of satisfaction) regarding 75 programs, but this ended in 2007 because it was difficult to reflect evaluation data in the budget. Tokyo also stopped evaluating administrative work in 2005 after implementing administrative evaluation in 1999. Local governments such as these actively tried to refine evaluation, but their approaches did not spread much to other local governments or become standard systems with a high level of versatility.

6 Relative Evaluation within an Organization

6.1 *The approach in Yao City, Osaka Prefecture*

Yao City is a government-designated city in central eastern Osaka Prefecture with a population of 270,000 people and a general account size of ¥89.9 billion (initial budget for FY 2011). In Yao City, a new comprehensive plan (basic concept: 10 years; basic plan: 5 years; implementation plan: 3 years) scheduled to begin in 2011 was formulated in FY 2010, and in the process of doing this, administrative business management required a comprehensive plan to be effectively realized.

Yao City had already implemented PPP evaluation system, but the implementation plan up to then did not properly define the relationship between the goals and responsibilities of each department clearly, so the responsibility for performance was vague. Thus, Yao City placed departmental management (as organization performance management) as a key element of the business management system and changed so that departmental management plays a leading role in the public meeting structure and decision-making process within agencies.

As shown in Fig. 1, ex-post administrative evaluations are used for sharing information at the department level for that year and the following

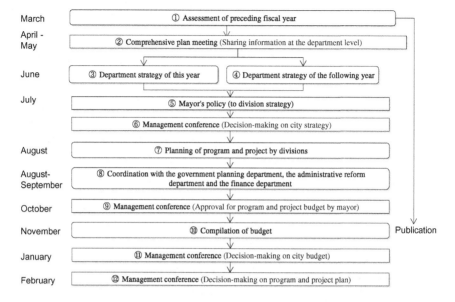

Fig. 1.   Organizational management flow in Yao City.
Source: Yao City (translated by the author)

year, and considering the strategy of the city as a whole, the departmental strategy for this year and the department strategy for the following year are formulated. Department strategy, considering the thoughts of the mayor, after inter-departmental adjustments, this is decided as the city's strategy, and departments consider measures for the following year and distribution of program and project resources, so after adjusting with the Policy Promotion Section, Administrative Reform Section, and Finance Section, and after the mayor's study, the specific budget-making phase is entered, and decisions on an initial budget and plans and business policies for the following year are made by the assembly.

A management sheet like the one in Fig. 2 was created in order to clarify the management performance responsibilities. This is an attempt to manage policy goals relating to the following year's business guidelines and to manage plans for component programs and projects, taking into consideration the long-term (10-year) departmental mission and medium-term (3-year) basic policy. As a result, the comprehensive plan can be expected to lead to plan achievement by developing plans for the following year in each department. In this process, evaluation data from the previous year is used when studying what direction to take in the current year and following year

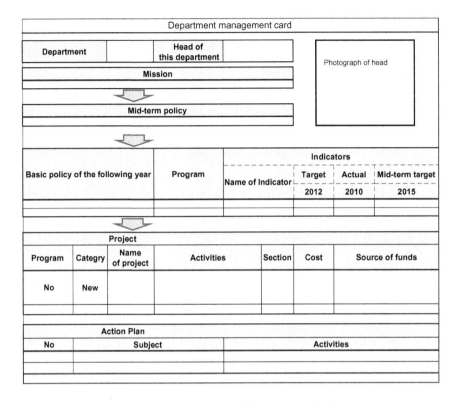

Fig. 2.   Departmental Management Card.
Source: Yao City (translated by the author)

at the beginning of the term. However, instead of functioning as the main organizational performance management system within an organization, the PPP evaluation system merely provides measurement and evaluation data to the organizational performance management system in line with the planning structure.

6.2   Administrative evaluation data and decision-making

In Yao City, progress has been made in the decentralization of planning and implementation, but not in the decentralization of budgeting. The city's financial condition is not in crisis, but it is not at all healthy either. Therefore, it is necessary to ensure that projects do not overlap among departments and to optimize everything by prioritizing from an agency-wide perspective. In addition, for each region, optimum distribution of resources

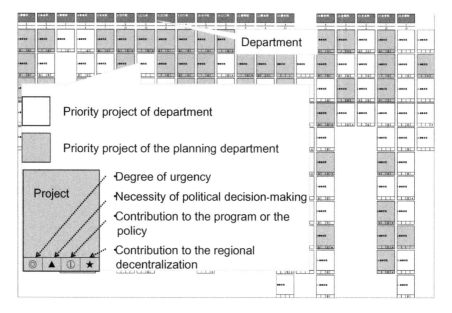

Fig. 3. Relative evaluation map in Yao City.
Source: Yao City (translated by the author)

is required. Therefore, sharing of information and discussions toward optimization are necessary among departments and with top city officials.

In Yao City, a chart-like relative evaluation map was made as a tool for
discussion among departments and with top city officials (Fig. 3). On the
map, each department, based on its objectives, arranges highly beneficial
approaches toward policy achievement in the order of priority, marks (cells
outlined in bold) Policy Planning Department Head proposals from the
perspective of city-wide optimization, and then the need and urgency of
decentralization and political decisions are determined for each project. Top
city officials and department heads understand how units think they should
distribute resources, and through discussion, they study which projects the
city as a whole should receive priority resource distribution.

7 Absolute Evaluation Outside the Organization

7.1 *Relevance with budget and account settlement*

This is an attempt to see administrative evaluation as a subsystem of the
budgeting and account settlement system of financial accounting. In Japan,

budgets are prescribed by law and must be categorized into subsections and paragraphs according to the purpose (Article 216 of the Local Autonomy Law). The subsections (e.g., general affairs expenditures, public welfare expenditures) and paragraphs (e.g., social welfare expenses, project welfare expenses) are not prescribed in detail and lack specificity. In addition, budgeting by program/project in accordance with planning systems is required by law. Therefore, accountability to residents is expected to be strengthened by disclosing the approximate amount requested for each program/project, account settlement data, cost data, and so forth, and by disclosing targets and actual figures for non-financial outcomes.

7.2   *Background of approaches in Itami City*

Itami City is a city with a population of 196,974 people (2008) and a general account size of ¥62.2 billion (2011 initial budget). Itami has implemented PPP evaluation since 2001, but has focused on reflecting this in the budget since 2004. In 2005, Itami strengthened the connection between program/project evaluation and budget-making, and starting in 2007, the city categorized evaluations into post-settlement evaluations based on previous year results and preliminary evaluations based on the direction of the coming year. Post-settlement evaluations are disclosed as supplementary materials to account settlement, and preliminary evaluations are disclosed as supplementary materials to the budget. Thus, a framework was built in which the budget and account settlement could be evaluated from the viewpoints of the comprehensive plan and the implementation plan.

7.3   *Framework for linking with budget and account settlement*

Figure 4 is a worksheet for preliminary evaluations done since 2007. Basically, one worksheet is prepared for each policy measure, and outcome benchmarks and five-year targets for the policy measure, activity benchmarks, and plans for the program/project components, and approximate amounts needed in the budget are listed. Thus, the budget in Itami's financial accounting is deployed to policy measures, programs/projects, and other budgets. By comparing this preliminary evaluation with the post-settlement evaluation done the following year, it is possible to do a before-after comparison of the amount of resources invested on a financial accounting basis and outcomes relating to non-financial benchmarks, and it

Code	2102	Program	Improvement of children's academic ability							

Goals	Result of assessment	Indicator of outcomes						Budget (thousand of Yen)		Next fiscal year, this program is
		Indicator	Final target	Result	Target (Next year)	Mid-term target	This year	Next year (estimate)	

Improvement of- · basic academic ability (math., mother tongue..) · Basic English skill · International communication skill	◎ (very good)	① achievement index for elementary school (Itami / national avg.)	101.00	95.70	100.00	101.00	152,821	159,609	**priority!**
		② achievement index for junior high school (Itami / national avg.)	101.00	101.30	100.00	101.00			
		③							
Vision of this year									

Related projects (components of this program)

code	Projects	Results	Indicator and target		Budget				trend of budget	process improvement	Degree of priority
			Indicator (unit)	target (this year)	target (next year)	This year (actual)	Next year (estimate)			
210201	A promotion of new educational program for reading, writing and hearing	☆☆☆☆	number of implemented school	11.00	17.00	104,850	114,425	↑	○	priority
210204	Support for English education for elementary school	☆☆☆	number of English teaching assistant	9.00	9.00	6,929	6,664	↓	—	keep
210206	Child supporter dispatch project	☆☆☆	number of registrant (N)	30.00	30.00	1,144	1,144	—	—	keep
210208	Support for English reference book	☆☆☆	number of distribution	2,000.00	2,300.00	988	2,431	↑	—	keep
210209	Support for English speech contest	☆☆	number of participator (N)	20.00	20.00	75	74	—	○	keep
210210	native speaker dispatch project	☆☆☆☆	number of day of class per school	60.00	60.00	27,146	22,276	↓	—	keep

Fig. 4. Worksheet for preliminary evaluations.

is possible to evaluate what results were obtained in respect of the amount of resources invested.

In Itami City, there was not much interest in the first one or two years after the implementation in 2007, but it gradually spread through the assembly, and now it is used more frequently in Q&A sessions at budget council meetings.

8 Relative Evaluation Outside

8.1 *Administrative evaluation and relative performance evaluation in Japan*

One factor that creates problems for establishing reasonable target levels is that in Japan there are no uniform systematic measurement criteria that focus on qualitative evaluation of administrative services, which makes relative evaluation among local governments difficult. The National Indicators

Set (NIS) and Best Value Performance Indicators (BVPIs) in the UK are typical examples of Relative Performance Evaluation (RPE). This implementation of relative performance management requires specialist knowledge and staff in order to interpret evaluation results and be used within an organization, but by demonstrating relative performance results among entities, each local government can evaluate its own performance in comparison with that of other local governments, which encourages learning, leads to improvement in efficiency and usefulness, and increasing accountability to residents. (Siverbo and Johansson, 2006, pp. 274–275; Kanemura, 2005, p. 130; Ministry of Home Affairs, Administration Bureau, 2000, p. 107, etc.)

In a study (2008) done by Matsuo (2009), approximately half (49%) of the 574 local government respondents in Japan think that relative evaluation would be good. However, in Japan, where there are no systematic standard benchmarks, many types of evaluation benchmarks are used by local governments. Table 3 shows what types of performance benchmarks are used in each administrative domain of six government-designated cities (Matsuo, 2010). This found that all of the cities apply performance evaluation to a relatively wide domain and use multiple types of benchmarks. In addition, it found that all of the cities differentiate between benchmarks according to the domain, and the methods of differentiation are diverse, as are the types of benchmarks used by cities even in the same domains. If the methods of using these diverse performance management benchmarks are regarded as reasonably established for each local government's purpose of using performance evaluation data, if voluntary relative evaluation is implemented as in Japan, there is likely to be a great need to either introduce comprehensive evaluation benchmarks or coordinate mutual evaluation items.

8.2   *Examples of relative performance evaluation approaches in Japan*

Thus, even in Japan, where there is an environment that permits diverse evaluation benchmarks without institutionalizing systematic, uniform relative evaluation benchmarks, there are several relative performance management approaches. The main approach is the one among member cities of the City Administrative Evaluation Network Conference established by the

Table 3.   Applications of performance measures in various public services.

Public services	Yokohama	Osaka	Nagoya	Kobe	Kyoto	Kawasaki
Police	1,3,4,5	1,3	1,3	1,2,3	1,2,3,5	1,3
Fire prevention/ suppression	1,3,4,5	1,3	1,2,3,4	1,2	1,2,3,5	1
Emergency medical services	1,3,4,5	1		1,2	1,2,3,5	1
Animal control	1,3,4,5		1,2,3	1,2	1,2,3,5	1,3
Community planning and zoning	1,3,4,5	1,3	1	1,2,3,5	1,2,3,5	1,4
Code enforcement/ inspection	1,3,4,5	1	1,3	1,2	1,2,3,5	1,3
Housing	1,3,4,5	1	1,2		1,2,3,5	1
Water supply/ sewerage	1,3,4,5	1,3	1,2,3,4,5	1,2	1,2,3,5	1,3
Solid waste collection/ disposal	1,3,4,5	1,3,5	1,2,3	1,2,3	1,2,3,5	1,3
Street maintenance/ construction	1,3,4,5	1,3	1,3		1,2,3,5	1
Traffic engineering	1,3,4,5				1,2,3,5	
Public transport	1,3,4,5	1	1,2,3,4,5	3	1,2,3,5	1,3
Public health hospitals	1,3,4,5	1,3,5	1,2	1	1,2,5	1
Libraries	1,3,4,5	1,3	1,2		1,2,3,5	
Parks & recreation	1,3,4,5	1,3	1,2	1,2,3	1,2,3,5	1,3
City attorney	1	1,3	1,3	1,2	1,2	
City clerk	1,3,4,5	1	1,2,3	1,2	1,2	
Purchasing	1,3,4,5	1	2	1,2	1,2	
Fleet maintenance	1,3,4,5	1	1,2		1,2	
Risk management	1,3,4,5	1,3	1,2,3	1,2,3	1,2,3	1
Data processing	1,3,4,5	1,3	1,2,3	1,2	1,2,3,5	1,3
Budget and finance					1,2	
Personnel/human resources			1,3	1,2	1,2	

(*Continued*)

Table 3. (*Continued*)

Public services	Yokohama	Osaka	Nagoya	Kobe	Kyoto	Kawasaki
Education	1,3,4,5	1,3	1,2,3	1,2,5	1,2,3,5	1,4,5
Social welfare service for elderly people	1,3,4,5	1,3	1,2,3	1,2,3	1,2,3,5	1,3
Social welfare service for handicapped people	1,3,4,5	1	1,2,3,4,5	1,2,3	1,2,3,5	1,3
Public programs for young people	1,3,4,5	1,3	1,2,3	1,2,3	1,2,3,5	1,3
Public programs for consumer	1,3,4,5	1,3	1,2,4,5	1,2	1,2,3,5	1
Art and culture	1,3,4,5	1,3,5	1,2,5	1,2,3	1,2,3,5	1
Tourism	1,3,4,5	1,3	1,2,3	1,3	1,2,3,5	3

Notes: 1 Workload or Output Measures, 2 Unit Cost or Efficiency Measures, 3 Outcomes or Effectiveness Measures, 4 Service Quality Measures, 5 Client or Citizen Satisfaction Measures.
Source: Matsuo, 2010.

National Institute for Research Advancement (NIRA) in 2005,[2] in which 86 entities participated (as of March 2009). In addition, there is an approach implemented primarily by local governments, such as the approaches of Fukui City and Ryugasaki City. Fukui's approach is a relative comparison of same-sized local governments throughout Japan, focusing on government-designated cities, and 34 entities participate as of 2006. Ryugasaki's approach was implemented in 2000 targeting eight neighboring cities and villages in the southern area of the prefecture. In addition, Zushi City, Fujisawa City, and Kamakura City have implemented an approach called "Shonan Benchmarking". NIRA benchmarks and model indicators used in "The Conference for Municipality Performance Evaluation" were standardized from the four viewpoints of basic benchmarks, results benchmarks, outcome benchmarks, and cost benchmarks for 24 programs/projects that have a great deal in common, such as children's daycare service, elderly care

---

[2]Transferred to independent research institutes (86 local governments, end of March 2009) under the Council of Regional Think Tanks, from FY 2009.

Table 4. Example of NIRA benchmark indicator (waste disposal service).

Type of indicator	Example of indicators
Basic indicator	Daily per capita weight of refuse (garbage disposal)
Output indicator	Daily per capita weight of incinerate, Utilization rate of use of remaining heat
Outcome indicator	Daily per capita weight of recycling, Recycling rate, Daily per capita weight of final disposal
Cost indicator	Daily per capita garbage disposal cost

Source: The Conference for Municipality Performance Evaluation, 2006.

service, and trash collection and disposal service. For example, trash collection and disposal service is composed of the benchmarks above (Table 4). Data from 80-odd cities were tallied for 24 projects, and for each city and item, the figures for the relevant city, national averages, highs, lows, and deviation were output. The existence of relative benchmarks is thought to increase objectivity and validity in goal setting and performance evaluation. In particular, in the examples described earlier, for independent systems, there is little risk of manipulation in order to arbitrarily make the figures look better. In addition, for the business management of participating local governments, evaluations focusing on highly reasonable benchmarks are possible, so flexibility is great.

9 Discussion

The earlier sections in this chapter organizes the challenges being faced by PPP evaluation in Japan and, through case studies, examines methods for overcoming these challenges.

First, for absolute evaluations within an organization, all of the local governments covered by Matsuo (2009) as advanced cases are facing challenges in reflecting overall evaluation data, particularly in decision-making within an organization, so they have stopped elaborative evaluation. Refinement of measurement standards and resident satisfaction evaluation are somewhat effective in that they increase the usefulness of evaluation data in decision-making. However, it may be wise to understand that it is difficult to provide versatile overall evaluation data for diverse decision-making within an organization.

For RPE (relative performance evaluation), in a model such as Ryugasaki, which makes comparisons with neighboring local governments, it is easy to explain the significance of comparing, but national comparisons between local governments with limited samples may be criticized that the validity if evaluation results is not very high. In this sense, as of now, their role as a reference for setting benchmarks and targets in each department is probably limited.

Yao City was given as an example of relative evaluation internally. In this case, as a result of emphasizing plan achievement, the challenge was how to manage each departmental organization, so the focus was on organizational performance management. Each department formed business objectives for the current year and the next year at the beginning of the term, and in the process of coordinating with other department heads and top city officials and reflecting this in decision-making for the budget, project-specific evaluation data from past years was only provided at the beginning of the term and thus was positioned as one piece of information for organizational performance management. In addition, Itami City was introduced as an example of absolute evaluation outside an organization. Post-settlement evaluation provides financial and non-financial outcome data on policy measures and projects implemented in the previous year to the account settlement council as supplementary material. Preliminary evaluation provides budget amounts and non-financial goal data on policy measures and projects scheduled to be implemented in the following year to the budget council. In this sense, Itami City's performance evaluation system is positioned to supplement the financial accounting system. These approaches were found to be useful in making decisions on PPP evaluation data based on the existence of organizational management and financial management systems, respectively.

10   Conclusion

PPP evaluation, the main NPM-related approach used by local governments in Japan, has been implemented by local governments throughout Japan since 2000, and even now implementation continues. Because there it was not legally mandatory, evaluation systems meeting the business management needs of local governments could be implemented, but benchmark comparability is poor, and depending on the design methods, the information is not very useful in decision-making. Even in fact-finding surveys, many local governments realize that it is difficult to reflect the information in budgets or otherwise use the information for management.

The following was found as a result of classifying and studying methods for increasing the usefulness in decision-making. The method of refining evaluation data within an organization cannot be regarded as meaningless, but the expected action outcomes may not be realized even if the system is streamlined, and a certain contribution could be made to measuring and evaluating the performance of departments and budget systems in line with the planning structure by incorporating into departmental management, budgeting, and other business management systems. However, PPP evaluation only functions to provide measurement and evaluation data in line with planning structure as a subsystem of budget or organization performance evaluation. If local governments that emphasize departmental management like Yao City increase, PPP evaluation will become embedded in the organizational performance management system within the administrative organization, and if the position in the budget/account settlement rises like in Itami City, PPP evaluation will become embedded in the budget and account settlement system. In this sense, the significance of administrative evaluation systems as business management systems will probably decline.

Of course, a fact-finding survey by questionnaire is necessary to determine whether this could become the trend for administrative evaluation systems in local governments, and the author would like to verify this direction based on the above discussion.

References

DiMaggio, P. J. and W. W. Powell (1983). The iron cage revisited: Institutional isomorphism and collective rationality in organizational fields, *American Sociological Review*, 48(2), 147–160.
Flynn, N. (1986). Performance measurement in public sector services, *Policy and Politics*, 14(3), 389–404.
Furukawa, S. and N. Kitaoji (2001). *Theory and Practice of Public Sector Assessment*, Tokyo: Nihon Kajo Shuppan Inc. (in Japanese).
Guthrie, J., O. Olson and C. Humphrey (1999). Debating developments in new public financial management: The limits of global theorising and some new ways forward, *Financial Accountability & Management*, 15(3–4), 209–228.
Kanemura, T (2005). A study on the practice administration assessment, 1, *Chiho-Zaimu*, 609, 129–141 (in Japanese).

Kelly, J. M. (2002). Why we should take performance measurement on faith, *Public Performance & Management Review*, 25(4), 375–380.

Lapsley, I. (1999). Accounting and the new public management: Instruments of substantive efficiency or a rationalising modernity? *Financial Accountability & Management*, 15(3–4), 201–207.

Matsuo, T. (2009). *Performance Evaluation System in Local Government*, Tokyo: Chuo-Keizai-sha Inc. (in Japanese).

Matsuo, T. (2010). A study on diversity and effectiveness of performance evaluation system in local governments, *Kokumin-Keizai Zasshi*, 202(2), 29–45 (in Japanese).

Ministry of Home Affairs (2000). *An Implementation Method of Performance Evaluation System in Local Government*, Tokyo: Ministry of Home Affairs (in Japanese).

Ministry of Public Management, Home Affairs, Posts and Telecommunications (2010). *A Survey on Actual Situation of the Policy-Program-Project Evaluation System in Japanese Local Governments*, Tokyo: Ministry of Public Management, Home Affairs, Posts and Telecommunications (in Japanese).

Osumi, S. (1999). *New Public Management*, Tokyo: Nippon-Hyoron-sha Co., Ltd. (in Japanese).

Poister, T. H. (2003). *Measuring Performance in Public and Nonprofit Organizations*, San Francisco, CA: Jossey-Bass.

Siverbo, S. and T. Johansson (2006). Relative performance evaluation in Swedish local government, *Financial Accountability & Management*, 22(3), 271–290.

The Conference for Municipality Performance Evaluation (2006). *Annual Report*, Tokyo: National Institute for Research Advancement (NIRA) (in Japanese).

Yamada, O. (2006). Why is the indicator used? A use of comparison-improvement cycle, *Kaikei-Kensa-Kenkyu*, 38, 75–85 (in Japanese).

Yamaguch, N. (2008). A study on functions of performance evaluation and system design in local government, *Kaikei-Kensa-Kenkyu*, 34, 17–32 (in Japanese).

Yamamoto, K. (2001). *Public Sector Accounting Reform*, Tokyo: Chuo-Keizai-sha Inc. (in Japanese).

8
Implementation of the Balanced Scorecard in the Japanese Prefectural Hospitals

Naoya Yamaguchi
Niigata University

1 Introduction

In recent years, Japanese hospitals have witnessed worsening problems such as a reduction in medical fees and a shortage and maldistribution of hospital doctors. Meanwhile, the number of hospitals implementing the Balanced Scorecard (BSC) is increasing year after year.

Previous studies on the implementation of the hospital BSC include Kaplan and Norton (2001), Pink *et al.* (2001), Inamdar and Kaplan (2002), Kocakülâh and Austill (2007), and Chang *et al.* (2008), etc. Kaplan and Norton (2001) described the implementations of the BSC in two U.S. hospitals: the Duke Children's Hospital and Montefiore Hospital. Pink *et al.* (2001) described a process of creating the BSC for the Ontario Province hospital system in Canada. Inamdar and Kaplan (2002) surveyed the implementation and effect of the BSC in nine U.S. healthcare provider organizations. Kocakülâh and Austill (2007) conducted a detailed analysis of the implementation of the BSC in a U.S. healthcare group and its main hospital. Chang *et al.* (2008) analyzed the performance improvement after implementing the BSC for a large hospital that first introduced the BSC in Taiwan.

Similar ones in Japan include Takahashi (2004), Arai (2005), Tani (2006), Ito (2006), and Japan Association for Healthcare Balanced Scorecard Studies (2007), etc. Of these, Takahashi (2004) and Arai (2005) conducted a detailed analysis of the implementation of the BSC in the Mie prefectural hospitals.

With the aim of improving the business performance of its prefectural hospitals, Niigata Prefecture began implementing the BSC in some hospitals from the 2004 fiscal year and in all 15 hospitals since the 2007 fiscal year. I engaged in activities that supported the implementation of the BSC in the hospitals as an advisor for BSC promotion in the 2007 fiscal year. This chapter conducts a case study on the implementation of the BSC in the Niigata prefectural hospitals as an example of Japanese prefectural hospitals, and attempts to describe its features and problems.

2 Features and Problems of the Japanese Medical System

National medical systems vary, and the system that is currently in operation has a strong influence on the management of the nation's hospitals. Therefore, it is necessary to first outline the Japanese medical system.

Palier (2004) classified the medical systems of advanced nations into the following three types: Public System, Medical Insurance System, and Free System. Of these, the Public System has the highest degree of involvement by the central government, while the Free System has the least involvement. The Japanese medical system belongs to the Medical Insurance System category. The following are the five features of this system: "compulsory public health insurance for all", "freedom of private practice by doctors", "freedom of access to all medical institutions", "payments at piece rates", and "control of medical expenditure and the achievement of policy objectives through the pricing of medical fees by the central government".

Compulsory public health insurance for all means that the central government has imposed a duty of entry to public health insurance on everyone in the nation. In Japan, there are various public health insurance providers associated with companies, trade associations, and residential areas, etc. Everyone in the nation is obliged to join the specified public health insurance applicable to their occupation, age, and residential area, etc. There are no differences among different types of health insurance in terms of both the coverage of medical services granted and the patient's fee. Every patient usually has to pay only 30% of the total medical fee. Moreover, since the maximum patients' payments for the high-priced medical care are set according to their income levels, if the total medical fee is expensive, the patient's payment will be kept low and the patient's health insurance will pay the rest of the medical fee to the medical institution.

Freedom of private practice by doctors means that every doctor is allowed to have his/her own medical practice anywhere, determine their own specialties freely, such as internal medicine, surgery, or pediatrics, and can examine patients at their own discretion (Ikegami, 2010).

Freedom of access to all medical institutions means that every patient can consult any doctor freely in any medical institution. In England, for primary care, every patient must first consult a general practitioner (GP) who is registered as their family doctor. In addition, for secondary and tertiary care, patients cannot consult any hospital doctor directly without a letter of introduction from their GP, except in an emergency. However, in Japan, for primary care, every patient can consult any practitioner or any hospital doctor directly, unless the hospital itself restricts the primary care treatment. Moreover, for secondary and tertiary care, any patient can consult any hospital doctor directly.

Payments at piece rates means that most medical fees are paid to the medical institutions at piece rates whenever they provide medical treatment, such as patient examinations, injections, or operations. Since the central government has set the medical fees for every individual course of medical treatment, the greater the number of medical treatments provided by a medical institution, the greater its income. However, since April 2003, an inclusive payment system called Diagnosis Procedure Combination (DPC) has been introduced mainly in the large hospitals. In DPC, the medical treatment fees are set for every diagnosis procedure combination involved in the course of medical treatment, except for operations, anesthesia, and radiotherapy.

Control of medical expenditure and the achievement of policy objectives through the pricing of medical fees by the central government implies that, by issuing a medical fee amendment every two years, the central government intends not only to control national medical expenses by restraining the extent of increases or reducing to the entire amendment but also requires all medical institutions to expand medical practices that are currently insufficient and to reduce the excessive ones by raising and reducing the medical fees, respectively (Ikegami, 2010).

3   Problems of the Medical Offer System in Japan

Various problems with the Japanese medical offer system have been indicated, and this chapter focuses on the following two important problems: "shortage of hospital doctors" and "insufficient functional specialization in hospitals".

3.1 *Shortage of hospital doctors*

With respect to the causes of the shortage of hospital doctors, the shortage in absolute numbers and the maldistribution of doctors are pointed out. In order to address the shortage in absolute numbers, the central government has, since the 2008 fiscal year, gradually increased the quota of medical students in all universities with medical departments.

There are two types of maldistribution: among specialties and among areas. With regard to maldistribution among specialties, since every doctor can freely set their own specialties, controlling the number of doctors in every specialty unit is difficult. Recently, there have been too few doctors in specialties that are at a high risk for lawsuits over malpractice, and those with severe working conditions, such as surgery, anesthesiology, obstetrics, gynecology, and pediatrics. With regard to maldistribution among areas, although the shortage of doctors in depopulated areas has been a serious problem for a long time, the university hospitals have dispatched their doctors to these areas in response to the requests of hospitals, particularly local government hospitals. However, since 2004, in the new clinical training system for doctors, every intern can freely select their training hospital and many have selected urban general hospitals. As a result, since the number of doctors in most university hospitals has decreased sharply, they have had to withdraw their doctors from hospitals in the depopulated areas. This has resulted in a serious shortage of doctors in many local government hospitals.

3.2 *Insufficient functional specialization in hospitals*

In Japan, the specialization of hospitals is insufficient, and this tendency is remarkable in large hospitals that mainly admit advanced secondary or tertiary care patients.

Many patients prefer large hospitals over clinics and tend to consult the doctors in large hospitals even for primary medical treatment. Furthermore, for these hospitals, primary care is an important source of income. In Japan, since the Japan Medical Association, whose membership mainly comprises practitioners, has had a strong influence on the setting of medical fees by the central government — the medical fees for outpatients have been treated more favorably than those for inpatients. Although this has contributed to the control of national medical expenses and patients' payments, the hospitals that mainly admit secondary or tertiary care patients have had worse financial performance.

Therefore, these hospitals must regard primary care as important because of their financial issues; however, this has caused both the deterioration of the quality of primary medical treatment in the hospitals, which is expressed with irony as "three hours of waiting and three minutes of medical treatment", and severe working conditions for the hospital doctors.

4   The State of Local Government Hospitals

The Medical Law of Japan classifies institutions with 20 beds or more as hospitals and those with 19 or fewer beds as clinics. The "Surveys of Medical Organizations Movement" by the Ministry of Health, Labor and Welfare found that the number of hospitals as of October 2009 was 7,655. Of these, the 272 national hospitals and 958 local government hospitals accounted for 16.1% of the total. The percentage of hospitals with 300 beds or more was 76% of the total number of national hospitals and 31% of the total number of local government hospitals. National hospitals mainly admit advanced secondary or tertiary care patients. Meanwhile, among the local government hospitals, there are not only many large hospitals that admit advanced secondary or tertiary care patients, but also many small or medium hospitals that admit emergency and disaster cases as well as patients from depopulated areas.

In most local government hospitals, the financial performance has worsened, which will ultimately result in financial difficulties for the local governments. In response to this, the Ministry of Internal Affairs and Communications released the "Local Government Hospitals Reform Guideline" in December 2007. This guideline requires integrated reforms based on the improvement of operating efficiency, reorganization and networking, and a review of management style.

5   Outline of Niigata Prefectural Hospitals

The territory of Niigata Prefecture is divided into seven secondary medical care areas; the maintenance and completeness of the medical structure for each area has been ensured in this prefecture. It has 15 prefectural hospitals, which is the second largest number among all 47 prefectural governments after Iwate.

These prefectural hospitals comprise three "Specialized Hospitals" (hospitals that specialize in certain functions), two "Broader-based Core Hospitals" (hospitals that contribute to the maintenance and completeness of the medical structure for areas containing two or more secondary areas), four "Local Core Hospitals" (hospitals that assume the core function of providing medical care in only one secondary area), and six "Community Hospitals" (hospitals that admit mainly primary care, subacute care, and home healthcare patients, and have the responsibility of maintaining the medical structure of a depopulated area through cooperation with the "Broader-based Core Hospitals"). Since Niigata Prefecture has the fifth largest area of all prefectures, and it has a lot of areas that experience heavy snowfall, there are distinctive features in that it has two or more prefectural hospitals in the same area and it has many "Community Hospitals" in the depopulated areas.

The environment surrounding the prefectural hospitals has increased the severity of factors, such as the suspension or closing of specialties caused by the serious shortage of doctors, reduction in medical fees, and reduction of population within the medical areas, all of which have worsened their financial performance further.

6   Features of the Balanced Scorecard in Niigata Prefectural Hospitals

6.1   *Outline of the balanced scorecard*

The Balanced Scorecard (BSC), developed by Robert S. Kaplan and David P. Norton, is a famous framework for strategic management (Kaplan and Norton, 1992, 1993, 1996a, 1996b, 2000, 2001, 2004). It proposes to make the visions and strategies of organizations and business units function by aligning them with targets and key performance indicators in four perspectives; financial, customer, internal business processes, and learning and growth.

When Kaplan and Norton introduced the BSC, they first intended to innovate on the traditional performance measurement systems. Subsequently, they came to regard the BSC as an integrated performance measurement system consistent with the visions and strategies. They emphasized the balance between financial and operational measures, the translation of strategies into specific measurable targets, and the clarification of cause-and-effect relationships among the four perspectives (Kaplan and Norton, 1996).

However, Kaplan and Norton have subsequently evolved the BSC into a strategic management system. They insisted that by using the BSC as the means of communication of strategies, the linkage between strategies and budgets, and the foundation of learning about strategies, the BSC will function as a system that promotes strategic management through the participation of all constituents. Moreover, they developed the Strategy Map as a framework for describing and visualizing strategies to enable the BSC to fulfill its function. They proposed the Strategy Map on the basis of the idea that the systematic description of strategies will increase the probability of their execution. According to Kaplan and Norton, the following four elements must be described on the Strategy Map: "Basic strategies" (earnings growth strategy and productivity strategy), "Customer Value Proposition", "Value-Creating Processes", and "Clustering of Assets and Activities" (Kaplan and Norton, 2004).

The author supports their views and regards the BSC not only as a performance measurement system but also as a strategic management system. The author gave advice to all hospitals on the basis of the idea that, as a prerequisite for developing their BSCs, it is essential to clarify their visions and strategies, and then to describe and visualize them on their Strategy Maps.

6.2 Features of the BSC in Niigata prefectural hospitals

The hospitals in Niigata prefecture name their BSC the "Management Sheet". It has a four-layer structure that comprises the director's sheet, department manager's sheets, section manager's sheets, and personal sheets. The features of the BSC in Niigata prefectural hospitals are presented in Fig. 1.

The "Management Sheet" has the following two features, which are the same as for Mie prefectural hospitals: First, Niigata prefectural hospitals place the "Customer Perspective" rather than the "Financial Perspective"

---

1. "Customer Perspective" is placed at the top as the final target.
2. It unites the Strategy Map and the BSC.
3. It emphasizes the cause-and-effect relationships among the four-layer sheets.
4. It is based on the vertical deployment approach.
5. It emphasizes the clarification of strategy on the director's sheet.
6. It is reviewed annually.

Fig. 1.   Features of the BSC in Niigata prefectural hospitals.

at the top of the BSC as the final target since they must retain unprofitable specialties in order to maintain the medical networks within their areas. However, since it is expected of them to retain their financial soundness in order to accomplish the target set in the "Customer Perspective", they place the "Financial Perspective" as the constraint in realizing their visions.

Second, the "Management Sheet" unites the Strategy Map and the BSC. It is essential for clarifying and visualizing the hospitals' strategies in their director's sheet, which is placed at the first layer of the BSC in order to fulfill its function as the strategic management system. Therefore, the style of the Management Sheet is one that unifies the Strategy Map and the BSC. The author required that all hospitals, in developing their BSCs, had to first review and clarify their strategies, then describe them on their Strategy Maps, and finally, describe their critical success factors, key performance indicators, and action plans. The author visited 14 of the 15 prefectural hospitals, interviewed and had discussions with each director and department managers, gave some advice for the director's sheet, and gave lectures to the personnel on the BSC.

In order to ensure the cause-and-effect relationships among the four-layer sheets, the Office of Prefectural Hospitals adopted the vertical deployment approach that first develops the director's sheet, and then gradually deploys the lower-layer sheets. The director's sheet is the most important point of strategy decision and the lower sheets are the important points of strategy execution. Therefore, the vector of the entire hospital must be clarified in the director's sheet, and then the vectors of the departments, sections, and personnel must be aligned with the vector of the entire hospital in the lower sheets.

The author made it clear to all hospitals that since the strategy decision in the director's sheet is extremely important, they have to clarify their strategies and describe them on their Strategy Maps in order to utilize the BSC for effective management without writing them merely as a ceremonious exercise. Moreover, the author insisted that it is necessary to review the Strategy Maps of the director's sheet at least annually in order to improve their abilities of strategy decision and communication.

7   Problems of the BSC in Niigata Prefectural Hospitals

The problems of the BSC will be shown under the headings: "strategy decision" and "deployment to the lower-layer sheets".

With regard to strategy decision, there were the following three problems: "lack of capability of the strategy decision", "insufficient consideration of strategy for strengthening the market responsiveness", and "focus on the internal specific functions exclusively for strengthening the specialization". Here, both market responsiveness and specialization are based on the classification of the strategies by Simons (2000).

First, *lack of capability of the strategy decision* means that, for the hospitals that have never thus far been managed on the basis of strategy, even if they are suddenly asked to clarify their strategies on their director's sheet, they cannot immediately deal with this, and even if they were to clarify their strategies, they could not describe them appropriately on their Strategy Maps.

Second, *consideration of strategy for strengthening the market responsiveness was insufficient* on the Strategy Maps of the director's sheet in most hospitals. Since the market responsiveness determines both the revenue base and necessary specialties, it is necessary for every hospital to review the function on which it concentrates according to the dynamics of population and other medical institutions within its area. Therefore, the author asked all hospitals to clarify the strategies for strengthening market responsiveness on their Strategy Maps.

Viewpoints for strengthening market responsiveness are: "Specialties" (internal medicine, surgery, etc.), "Phase of Care" (primary, secondary, tertiary), "Kind of Patients" (outpatients, inpatients, home patients), and "Stage of Illness" (acute, subacute, chronic, terminal). The decision about which segments each hospital should strengthen will be dependent on several factors, such as resources, dynamics of population, medical needs, and dynamics of competitors and cooperators. In order to strengthen market responsiveness, it is necessary for each hospital to identify the most important segment in alignment with its competitive position.

Third, *focus on the internal specific functions exclusively for strengthening the specialization* means that although most Strategy Maps on the director's sheets were much more conscious about specialization than market responsiveness, they focused exclusively on strengthening internal specific functions. Since a high degree of specialization is required in every hospital and it is the basis on which every patient relies on any hospital, it is essential to constantly maintain and strengthen the hospital's specialization. However, any mere mixture of sub-optimization could not lead to total optimization, and so every hospital must simultaneously pursue the total optimization as well as optimization of each department and section.

Here, total optimization means both that of the organization itself and in its association with other organizations.

Therefore, "strengthening some specializations of each department and section", "strengthening some specializations based on the cooperation among departments and among sections", "strengthening some hospital functions in association with other medical institutions", and "strengthening the present and future necessary specialties", will be mentioned as the viewpoints of specialization. There will be a tendency toward the viewpoint of specific functional enhancement only by a collection of functional strategies for every specialty, such as doctors, nurses, and other healthcare workers. In order to greatly improve the quality of medical services, it is necessary to strengthen not only the specific functions of each specialty, but also the functions of the entire hospital that are based on both the cooperation within the hospital itself and with other medical institutions, such as the improvement of patient services and total care through all stages of illness.

Then, for total optimization, it will be crucial to revitalize the communication among sections, departments, and organizations. Therefore, it is necessary to discuss and clarify aspects of the BSC with regard to both cooperation within the hospital itself and with other medical institutions, and the visions and action plans for the specialties necessary in the present and future.

Moreover, in order to strengthen both the market responsiveness and specialization, both "competition" and "cooperation" are extremely important. The perspectives are mentioned in Table 1. For market responsiveness, the perspective of competition is "Differentiation", and the one of cooperation is "Mutual Complement". For specialization, the perspective of competition is "Benchmarking" and the one of cooperation is "Total Optimization".

In the deployment to the lower-layer sheets, the following five problems were encountered.

(1) *The cause-and-effect relationships among the four-layer sheets were not secured.*

In order to execute the hospital strategies that are clarified on the director's sheet, it is necessary to secure the cause-and-effect relationships among the four-layer sheets in the sense that the strategic themes, strategic targets, and action plans clarified on the lower-layer sheets must contribute to

Table 1. Perspectives of hospital strategies.

Perspective Strategy	Competition	Cooperation
Market responsiveness	*Differentiation* — Can the main domain both satisfy the medical needs within the area and differentiate with other hospitals? — What is the strength in the domain of competing with other hospitals?	*Mutual complement* — How is cooperation with other medical institutions necessary to strengthen the capabilities of the main domain? — How is cooperation with other medical institutions necessary to complement the weakness in the main domain?
Specialization	*Benchmarking* — Are the specialties of the entire hospital sufficient in comparison with other hospitals? — Are the specialties of any department and section sufficient in comparison with others?	*Total optimization* — How is cooperation among internal departments or sections necessary to improve the patient services and total care? — How is cooperation with other medical institutions necessary to improve the patient services and total care?

the execution of strategic themes and the achievement of strategic targets of the higher-layer sheets. However, in many cases, the director's sheet, department manager's sheets, and section manager's sheets were made simultaneously without an awareness of the cause-and-effect relationships.

(2) *Many doctors were not cooperative.*

As also seen generally in previous studies, in most prefectural hospitals, the doctors' support and participation were not forthcoming in the deployment to the lower-layer sheets. Factors such as the shortage of doctors, severe working conditions, a lack of the sense of belonging to their hospitals, and antipathies against the BSC are mentioned as reasons.

However, the doctors assume central roles in most medical practices, and the nurses and other healthcare workers can only take on roles that support the doctors and follow the doctors' directions. Therefore, any BSC made only by the nurses and other healthcare workers without the cooperation of doctors is merely a rehash of the Management by Objectives (MBO) that each section of the nurses and other healthcare workers has implemented thus far.

Therefore, it is impossible to deploy strategies to the entire hospital with such a BSC. Moreover, it is impossible not only to show visions for strengthening the market responsiveness, but also to incorporate the functional strategies on the basis of cooperation among departments and sections and with other organizations.

(3) *Many personnels lacked a sense of belonging to the hospitals.*

In order to maintain the medical network within its territory, the Niigata Prefecture establishes its hospitals not only in urban areas but also in depopulated areas. Moreover, since it reshuffles personnels periodically to ensure that the hospitals located in depopulated areas have stable staff levels, most personnels except doctors have to change hospitals every few years. Therefore, many personnels find it difficult to develop a sense of belonging to the hospitals, and this would be a factor that might explain why their commitment to participating in the management by BSC is at a low level.

(4) *The management function was weak.*

In order to reduce staffing costs, the Niigata prefectural hospitals have gradually reduced the number of full-time employees who are involved in indirect work by employing part-timers or outsourcing medical assistance work.

However, for successful management by BSC, talented management staff who fully support the BSC are required. If the hospitals are prevented from securing them because of the staffing costs, this would be a determinant for preventing them from introducing the BSC.

The Office of Prefectural Hospitals has continuously trained several staff at each hospital to be BSC facilitators. Most of them are in medical professions such as nurses and other healthcare workers, except doctors, and they have taken great pains to obtain the cooperation of other medical professions.

(5) *There was no incentive to improve business performance on the basis of the BSC.*

The Office of Prefectural Hospitals adopts the same systems as those of the government itself for budgeting and personnel management. These include systems allocating wages in proportion to seniority and guaranteeing recognition of personnel status. Regardless of good or bad hospital performance, both their status and salaries will be guaranteed. As a result, this may have reduced the motivation for improved management on the basis of the BSC.

8 Conclusion

In response to severe financial difficulties, most local government hospitals are required to change their management radically. While the reorganization, networking, and change of management style that are required by the "Local Government Hospitals Reform Guideline" can be compared to "surgical procedures", the strategic management by BSC based on self-reliant efforts, can be compared to "internal medical procedures".

In order to implement management reforms, it is necessary to combine human elements, such as the director's strong leadership, doctors' participation and cooperation, reservation and training of talented staff supporting BSC management, and strong commitment of all staff for improved management. Furthermore, the creating of Strategy Map and the BSC is only the first step in the strategic management by BSC. They are meaningless unless the BSC gives rise to the actions required to improve management. It is expected that the efforts of BSC management would not end with merely the writing of BSC, but that they would lead to substantial improvement of strategic management.

In Japan, prefectural hospitals have the important mission of providing indispensable medical services for local residents. Therefore, they have to cope with two directly-opposed targets: *their financial soundness* and *the maintenance of universal services.* The author expects that the management by BSC should contribute to the achievement of both targets.

References

Arai, K. (2005). *Medical Balanced Scorecard*, Chuokeizai-sha, Inc (in Japanese).
Chang, W. C., Y. C. Tung, C. H. Huang and M. C. Yang (2008). Performance improvement after implementing the Balanced Scorecard:

A large hospital's experience in Taiwan, *Total Quality Management*, 19(11), 1143–1154.

Inamdar, N. and R. S. Kaplan (2002). Applying the Balanced Scorecard in healthcare provider organizations, *Journal of Healthcare Management*, 47(3), 179–195.

Ikegami, N. (2010). *Medical Problems*, Nikkei Publishing Inc. (in Japanese).

Ito, K. (2006). Case of introduction of strategy map and BSC, *Kigyo-Kaikei*, 58(10), 104–113 (in Japanese).

Japan Association for Healthcare Balanced Scorecard Studies (2007). *Complete Guide of the Balanced Scorecard for Healthcare Organizations*, Japan Productivity Center (in Japanese).

Kaplan, R. S. and D. P. Norton (1992). The balanced scorecard measures that drive performance, *Harvard Business Review*, 70(1), 71–79.

Kaplan, R. S. and D. P. Norton (1993). Putting the Balanced Scorecard to work, *Harvard Business Review*, 71(5), 134–142.

Kaplan, R. S. and D. P. Norton (1996a). Using the Balanced Scorecard as a strategic management system, *Harvard Business Review*, 74(1), 75–85.

Kaplan, R. S. and D. P. Norton (1996b). *The Balanced Scorecard: Translating Strategy into Action*, Harvard Business School Press.

Kaplan, R. S. and D. P. Norton (2000). Having trouble with your strategy? Then map it, *Harvard Business Review*, 78(5), 167–176.

Kaplan, R. S. and D. P. Norton (2001). *The Strategy-Focused Organization*, Harvard Business School Press.

Kaplan, R. S. and D. P. Norton (2004). *Strategy Maps*, Harvard Business School Press.

Kocakülâh, M. C. and A. D. Austill (2007). Balanced Scorecard application in the healthcare industry: A case study, *Journal of Health Care Finance*, 34(1), 72–99.

Palier, B. (2004). *La Réforme des systèmes de santé*, Press Universitaires de France.

Pink, G. H., I. McKillop, E. G. Schraa, C. Preyra, C. Montgomery and G. R. Baker (2001), Creating a balanced scorecard for a hospital system, *Journal of Health Care Finance*, 27(3), 1–20.

Simons, R. (2000). *Performance Measurement & Control Systems for Implementing Strategy*, Prentice Hall.

Society for Research of Management of Local Government Hospitals (2010). *Handbook of Management of Local Government Hospitals*, 12th edn., Gyosei (in Japanese).

Takahashi, T. (2004). *Strategic Management of Health Care Organizations: The Balanced Scorecard for Hospitals*, Japan Productivity Center (in Japanese).

Tani, T. (2006). Introduction of BSC to hospital management, *Kaikei*, 169(2), 52–70 (in Japanese).

9

Pricing Policy and Potential Cost Reduction in Telecommunications

Manabu Takano

Seinan Gakuin University

1   Introduction

Manufacturing and non-manufacturing industries in the West practice Activity-Based Costing (ABC) and Activity-Based Management (ABM), costing models which are also observed within the telecommunications sector — a public utility.[1] As fierce competition became widespread within each country's telecommunications industry in the West, ABC and/or ABM were further implemented in each domestic sub-sector, to enhance cost and workflow management. Similarly, the Japanese telecommunications industry introduced ABC to determine interconnectivity fee rates, beginning in FY 1998; however from FY 2000, these rates were calculated adopting the Long Run Incremental Costs (LRIC) model. Thus the adoption of LIRC, instead of actual expenses, made possible a sharp reduction in interconnectivity fees. However, when the LRIC model was first introduced, Nippon Telegraph and Telephone East Corporation and Nippon Telegraph and Telephone West Corporation (NTT East and West), companies responsible for telecommunications interconnectivity, incurred sizable sunk costs. Nevertheless, NTT East and West currently do not incur such sunk costs, but many fear such costs may relapse in the future. NTT East and West need to reduce actual expenses to prevent sunk costs from reoccurring in the future.

This chapter explores both the determination of interconnectivity fees in the Japanese telecommunications industry as well as the possibility of

---

[1]For example, Gwynne and Ashworth (1993), Terrence, Thomson, and Sharman (1994).

implementing ABM using ABC information at NTT East and West, to avoid sunk costs from reoccurring.

2 Interconnectivity Fees and "Connection Accounting"

2.1 *Outline of interconnectivity fees*

Nippon Telegraph and Telephone Corporation (NTT) was created through the privatization of Nippon Telegraph and Telephone Public Corporation in 1985. Simultaneously, the principle of market competition was introduced into the Japanese telecommunications industry. Thus, new common carriers (NCCs) entered the lucrative long-distance communications market.

NCCs, to offer long-distance communications services, had to both own their own telecommunication line as well as connect to either NTT's Group Unit Center (GC) or Intrazone Tandem Center (IC), as illustrated in Fig. 1. Since the lines in the A–IC segment and the B–IC segment were owned exclusively by NTT, NCCs were required to connect their own telecommunications line to NTT's exchange, when providing long-distance communications services. Interconnectivity fees are those paid by NCCs to NTT as compensation for this connection. Since interconnectivity fees represented revenue to NTT and expenses to NCCs, the interests of both parties were conflicting. If these fees were reduced, NCCs could cut their telecom fees, thus boosting competition further in the telecommunications market. Increased competition would probably lead to cheaper telecom fees, benefiting end-users.

2.2 *ABC and the implementation of "connection accounting"*

In the beginning, NTT applied regional communication fees to interconnectivity, although in 1994 it started calculating interconnectivity

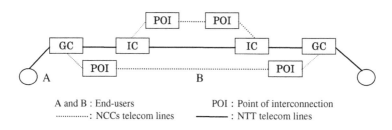

A and B : End-users   POI : Point of interconnection
············· : NCCs telecom lines   ———— : NTT telecom lines

Fig. 1.   Interconnectivity in the telecommunications industry.
Source: Fuke, 2000.

fees on the basis of NTT's profit center approach to revenue and expenses. At the time, however, there was no statute that clearly defined the conditions for interconnectivity and the method for calculating interconnectivity fees. NTT and NCCs, hence, engaged in laborious fee negotiations annually (Fuke, 2000). Thus the need emerged for a set of connectivity rules to be established, to ensure fair and effective competition between NTT and NCCs, which lead to the introduction of "connection accounting" in FY 1998.

"Connection accounting" is an accounting system required by telecommunications industry regulations. According to this system, NTT East and West are required to calculate and publish their revenue, expenses, and other information on telecom equipment related to connectivity as well as provide basic data on interconnectivity fees. "Connection accounting" is divided into "Category 1 Designated Equipment Management Division" (Management Division), which deals with telecom equipment and its management and operation, and "Category 1 Designated Equipment Usage Division" (Usage Division), which deals with telecom service sales. Interconnectivity fees were calculated by first adding borrowed and proprietary capital expenses and income taxes to Management Division expenses, excluding all Usage Division expenses unrelated to connectivity, and then dividing that by projected telecom volume.

The introduction of "connection accounting", has led to higher transparency in the interconnectivity fee calculation methodology; fees are determined on the basis of costs. ABC is also applied in "connection accounting" to calculate costs that form the basis for interconnectivity fees in a more rational method.

3 ABC in "Connection Accounting"

3.1 *Cost allocation flow*

Similar to other public utilities, telecommunications has large indirect/ shared expenses, in addition to it being an apparatus industry. These expenses are not necessarily linked to capacity-related activity drivers, such as the number of telecom lines and fixed asset values (Bussey, 1993). "Connection accounting" provides the cost information that interconnectivity fees are based on by applying ABC, which reflects the actual costs incurred when expenses are attributed to each respective equipment category as much as possible.

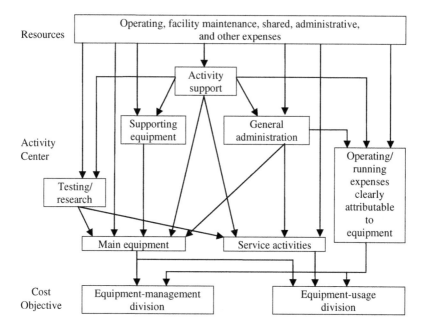

Fig. 2.   ABC cost allocation flow within "connection accounting".
Source: Compiled by the author on the basis of NTT West, 2010.

As illustrated in Fig. 2, ABC in "connection accounting" first compiles the resource-equivalent expenses incurred by each activity center, and then allocates these from the activity centers to both the Management Division and the equipment section within the Usage Division, which are subject to cost calculation. This cost allocation occurs in three stages as explained below.

The first stage is calculating expenses for each activity center. These expenses include operating expenses, running expenses, facility maintenance expenses, administrative expenses, testing and research expenses, depreciation and amortization expenses, fixed asset disposal expenses, and income tax expenses. On the other hand, activity centers are divided into calculation units corresponding to a business activity or asset class, and comprise the six categories of "main equipment", "supporting equipment", "operating/running expenses clearly attributable to equipment", "testing/ research", "general administration", and "service activities", as well as "activity support", which encompasses shared expenses relating to two or more of these activity centers (NTT West, 2010). These expenses are allocated to each activity center by a resource driver, i.e., proportional to an occupied area and/or net fixed assets. "Activity support" expenses are allocated to the related activity center based on things such as occupied area and number of active personnel.

The second stage is allocating the expenses calculated for "supporting equipment", "general administration", and "testing/research" into "main equipment," "service activities", and "operating/running expenses clearly attributable to equipment". "Supporting equipment" is allocated into "main equipment" only; "general administration" is allocated into "main equipment", "service activities", and "operating/running expenses clearly attributable to equipment"; and "testing/research" is allocated into "main equipment" and "service activities". ABC within "connection accounting" uses the term "cost driver" to describe this allocation standard. The expenses calculated for "support equipment", "general administration", and "testing/research" are allocated to each activity center by the cost drivers, as outlined in Table 1.

The third stage is allocating the expenses calculated for "main equipment", "service activities", and "operating/running expenses clearly

Table 1.   Cost driver examples.

Activity center	Activity	Cost driver
Supporting equipment	General supervision	Number of supervisory response cases
	Test receipt	Proportion of malfunctions
	Electrical equipment	Proportion of power usage in specifications
General administration	Material duties	Proportion of fixed assets acquired in the current fiscal year
	General/Welfare/HR	Proportion of revenue and expenses
	Training	Proportion of active personnels
Testing/research	Communications network structure	Proportion of fixed assets acquired in the current fiscal year
	Communications buildings	Proportion of area occupied
	Electrical devices for communications	Proportion of power usage in specifications

Source: See Fig. 2.

attributable to equipment" to both the Management Division and the equipment section within the Usage Division, which are subject to cost calculation. The expenses calculated for "main equipment" and "operating/ running expenses clearly attributable to equipment" are allocated to the Management Division and each equipment section within the Usage Division. Conversely, the expenses calculated for "service activities" are allocated only to the Usage Division. Allocations made during this stage are attributed to each equipment section in proportion to the number of telecom lines, the value of fixed assets acquired, and traffic, among other things.

3.2 Characteristics of ABC within "connection accounting"

The following three points can be given as characteristics of ABC within "connection accounting".

First, it considers telecommunications equipment as activities/activity centers. Among the six activity centers mentioned earlier, "main equipment" and "supporting equipment" fall under this category. The equipment that comprises the telecommunications network is a cost pool for "main equipment", and duties and/or equipment that support the main equipment are a cost pool for "support equipment". Considering telecommunications equipment as an activity may seem strange, since such equipment is normally a fixed asset. The activities considered here can be acknowledged; however, they denote the administrative and operational tasks necessary for telecommunications equipment and are delegated to each individual unit.

Second, "support equipment" and "general administration" are positioned as intermediate activity centers. Under normal ABC, cost allocation is a two-step process, in which resource costs are first compiled by activity and then allocated to those sections subject to cost calculation. In ABC under "connection accounting", expenses are allocated in a three-step process. The process includes "support equipment", which encompasses expenses related to network support, and "general administration", which encompasses expenses related to shared administrative tasks that are treated as intermediate activity centers. Since many supporting systems as well as administrative tasks are shared when providing telecommunications services, "support equipment", and "general administration" are established as intermediary activity centers. This enables a more rational allocation of expenses.

Third is the use of the term "cost driver" — corresponding to activity drivers — as the word that describes the standards used when allocating activity costs calculated for "supporting equipment", "general administration", and "testing/research" to "main equipment", "service activities", and "operating/running expenses clearly attributable to equipment". Activity drivers are the cost drivers utilized when allocating the costs calculated for each activity to each section, subject to cost calculation. (Raffish and Turney, 1991) "Cost drivers" are implemented in "connection accounting" when allocating costs from intermediate activity centers to main activity centers. Thus, the terminology is used in a different manner than normal ABC.

4 Application of the Long-Run Incremental Cost System and the Occurrence of Sunk Costs

4.1 *Application of the long-run incremental cost system*

The implementation of "connection accounting" made the methodology for interconnectivity fee calculation more straightforward, creating expectations of a subsequent sharp decline in interconnectivity fees. As illustrated in Table 2, however, even after the introduction of "connection accounting" in FY 1998, there was no such decline. In addition, the internationally high level of Japan's interconnectivity fees prompted foreign telecommunications providers and governments, particularly the U.S. government, to strongly urge a dramatic reduction in these fees. In response, the LRIC model was introduced in FY 2000 as a new methodology for calculating interconnectivity fees.

The LRIC model was a method for calculating interconnectivity fees that was based not on the actual expenses incurred by NTT East and West's existing network, but rather on the theoretical amount that the companies would spend if they constructed a completely new network using the cheapest and most efficient equipment and technology available at the time. If interconnectivity fees were calculated using the existing network of NTT East and West, the expenses arising from the previous inefficient management of the companies — including overhiring and excess capital expenditure — would be reflected in the fee calculation. Thus, large declines were not observed in interconnectivity fees, despite the implementation of "connection accounting". Since the LRIC method includes the competitive network projected to be developmental in the future model, although an analog exchange is actually used for a subscriber exchange, it would assume the usage of a cheaper and more efficient digital exchange.

Table 2.   Interconnectivity fee trends (price per 3-minute, in yen).

	Fiscal year								
	1994	1995	1996	1997	1998	1999	2000	2001	2002
	NTT profit center expenditure/revenue basis				"Connection accounting"		LRIC model		
IC connection	19.78	16.45	14.48	12.93	11.98	10.64	7.65	5.88	4.78
GC connection				6.31	6.19	5.81	5.57	4.95	4.60	4.50

	Fiscal year								
	2003	2004	2005	2006	2007	2008	2009	2010	2011
	LRIC model								
IC connection	5.79	6.12	7.09	6.84	6.55	6.41	6.38	6.96	6.57
GC connection	4.80	5.13	5.32	5.05	4.69	4.53	4.52	5.21	5.08

Source: Information and Communications Council Report, 2010.

Application of the LRIC model resulted in a large decline in interconnectivity fees. Table 2 illustrates that when the companies used the lump cost method that included actual expenses, IC connections were 10.64 yen and GC connections were 5.57 yen in FY 1999, which declined to 5.57 yen and 4.95 yen, respectively, when the LRIC model was introduced in FY 2000.

4.2 *Occurrence of sunk costs*

Many were anxious that since interconnectivity fees were calculated on the basis of LRIC rather than actual expenses, NTT East and West would incur a sunk cost for the amount they had already invested in their existing landline network, which partially could not be recovered.

Table 3 illustrates that NTT East and West incurred a sunk cost of 211.4 billion yen in FY 2001 and 13.3 billion yen in FY 2002, since actual expenses were greater than LRIC in these two years. However, this trend reversed in FY 2003 when LRIC became more than actual expenses, and since, sunk

Table 3.   Difference between LRIC and actual expenses in interconnectivity fee calculation (billion yen).

	Fiscal year				
	2001	2002	2003	2004	2005
LRIC	855.9	855.9	806.5	790.6	705.9
Actual expense	1,067.3	869.2	767.4	699.0	626.3
Difference (Sunk cost)	▲211.4	▲13.3	39.1	91.6	79.6
Accumulated sunk costs	211.4	224.7	185.6	94.0	14.4

	Fiscal year				
	2006	2007	2008	2009	2010
LRIC	666.4	620.6	568.4	509.3	455.2
Actual expense	594.7	525.0	464.2	431.8	410.9
Difference (Sunk cost)	71.7	95.6	104.2	77.5	44.3
Accumulated sunk costs	▲57.3	▲152.9	▲257.1	▲334.6	▲378.9

Source: See Table 2.

costs have not been incurred. As such, the sunk costs previously incurred by NTT East and West were completely recovered in FY 2006. The reason sunk costs were eliminated beginning in FY 2003 is because NTT East and West heavily curbed investment in their landline network. In their "NTT Group Three-Year Management Plan", for FY 2002 to 2004, the companies outlined a sharp shift in investment from their landline network to their optical fiber network, and drastically curtailed new capital expenditures in the former. (*Nihon Keizai Shimbun*, 2002) Without any new investment in the landline network, related expenses such as depreciation and amortization could not grow; thus actual expenses decreased. Conversely, since the LRIC model assumed that NTT East and West reconstructed their network, given continuous business operation of the companies, it did not account for reduced capital expenditures in the landline network; thus LRIC was higher than actual expenses.

The difference between LRIC and actual expenses was also disclosed by an expense category, beginning in FY 2007. Table 4 illustrates that the main cost factors that drove LRIC to exceed actual expenses included

Table 4. Gap between LRIC and actual expenses (by expense category) (billion yen).

	FY 2009			FY 2010		
	LRIC	Actual expenses	Difference	LRIC	Actual expenses	Difference
Operating expense	0.03	0.02	0.01	0.04	0	0.04
Facility maintenance expense	150.5	165.2	▲14.7	135.8	157.3	▲21.5
Shared and administrative expense	23.4	33.0	▲9.6	21.0	31.9	▲10.9
Testing and research expense	12.4	22.9	▲10.5	10.9	22.7	▲11.8
Depreciation and amortization expenses	211.9	123.1	88.8	188.6	114.0	74.6
Fixed asset disposal expense	6.7	8.9	▲2.2	5.8	10.7	▲5.0
Communications equipment usage fees	2.4	10.0	▲7.6	2.4	9.4	▲7.0
Income tax expense	18.2	18.2	0	16.3	17.6	▲1.4
Proprietary capital usage	83.8	50.5	33.3	74.4	47.3	27.1
Total	509.3	431.8	77.5	455.2	410.9	44.3

Source: Compiled by the author on the basis of NTT West, 2010.

depreciation and proprietary capital expense. Although the effect of these expenses was significant, the Information and Communications Council notes that NTT East and West are scheduled to replace their exchanges by FY 2015, and therefore, a strong probability exists that the downward trend in actual depreciation expenses will taper off and the gap between LRIC and actual expenses will shrink (Information and Communications Council, 2010). Under these circumstances, sunk costs may rematerialize for NTT East and West, as they did when the LRIC model was first applied. To prevent this, NTT East and West will probably need to reduce facility maintenance expenses, shared and administrative expenses, testing and research expenses, fixed asset disposal expenses, and communications equipment usage fee costs, actual expenses which are all currently larger

Table 5.   Expenses requiring reduction and attributed activity centers.

Expense	Attributed activity center
Facility maintenance expense	"Main equipment", "Support equipment", and "Activity support"
Shared and administrative expense	"General administration" and "Activity support"
Testing and research expense	"Testing/research"
Fixed asset disposal expense	"Main equipment", "Support equipment", and "Activity support"
Communications equipment usage fees	"Activity support"

Source: Compiled by the author on the basis of NTT West, 2010.

than LRIC. Since NTT East and West apply ABC within "connection accounting", these expenses can probably be lowered by switching from ABC to ABM.

5   Potential Cost Reductions in "Connection Accounting"

When lowering expenses, whose actual costs exceed LRIC, companies must first understand in which activity center each expense occurs. Since NTT East and West apply ABC in "connection accounting", they can identify occurring expenses by using ABC information. For instance, Table 5 illustrates that facility maintenance expenses are attributed to "main equipment", "support equipment", and "activity support". Thus, certain factor exists that causes facility maintenance expenses to occur in each of these activity centers. Once the companies identify where these expenses occur, they implement the ABM steps of activity analysis, cost driver analysis, and performance analysis within each relevant activity sector (Turney, 1992).

The first step is conducting an activity analysis to discover opportunities for cost improvement. Since the locations of expenses that have room for improvement have been identified, the companies conduct an activity analysis in the activity centers where the expenses occur. Moreover, since NTT East and West use ABC in "connection accounting", they first categorize activities according to those used in ABC (refer to Fig. 3). For instance, "supporting equipment" categorizes activities into general supervision, test receipt, and electrical equipment, among others. However, discovering opportunities for cost improvement is impossible by categorizing activities using ABC alone, as the overall scope of activities is too wide. It is therefore necessary to conduct a further cross-sectional, functional reassessment of activity categories used in ABC from a work process perspective, and break them down to activities that have a coordinated, mutual, linked relationship.[2] The activities were further divided into subcategories associated with work processes, enabling the companies to separate them into value-added activities necessary for interconnection and non-value added activities unnecessary for interconnection.

The completion of activity analysis is followed by the cost driver analysis. However, simply segregating activities into value-added and non–value-added through an activity analysis, does not by itself lead to reduced costs. The companies must identify the cost drivers for each of these activities, which are the factors that create cost. Discovering what these cost drivers involve, permits searching for cost elements by associating them with the activity subcategories, created in the activity analysis. For non–value-added activities, the companies revamp work processes to reduce costs by rooting out waste elements and investigating why these elements exist in the first place. For value-added activities as well, companies can cut activity costs by identifying the cost drivers and increasing efficiency to shrink the size of these as much as possible.

The final step is conducting a performance analysis to measure whether activities are being carried out efficiently and effectively. Here the companies analyze performance by dividing activity costs by the cost drivers, and then comparing it to a base value. Comparing these values to a benchmark is not possible for interconnection in the Japanese telecommunications industry, as NTT East and West are the only players in this business line. Nevertheless, a performance analysis is possible by allocating the LRIC calculated within that model to each activity identified in the activity analysis, making per-unit activity output the target and comparing this with actual performance. This process enables the companies to understand the gap between the LRIC target and actual performance. On the other hand, focusing on

---

[2]When conducting ABM, U.K. telecommunications firm, Mercury Communications, subdivided activities to a level in which an activity analysis was possible by utilizing the linked-value method.

the amount of activity cost reduction, which is the ultimate goal, as well as establishing performance evaluation standards for the cost drivers themselves, provides an easy-to-understand indicator for those carrying out the activities. This may produce effects that motivates such people to reduce activity costs.

Conducting the above ABM is a way of reducing operational costs at the interconnection service provision stage, however, it can also have a great impact on the outcome of cost reduction in the interconnection planning stage. As mentioned, interconnection-related costs were heavily influenced by NTT's medium-term management plan. Drawing up a plan that leads to cost reduction in NTT's medium-term management plan, which amounts to the interconnectivity planning stage, is therefore absolutely vital.

6 Conclusion

This chapter examined the method for determining interconnectivity fees in the Japanese telecommunications industry, with particular focus on "ABC within connection accounting", as well as the possibility for applying ABM using such ABC information.

Introducing ABC-applied "connection accounting", not only enables interconnectivity fees to be calculated in a more rational way than the previous fee-setting methodology but also ensures a more transparent calculation process. Characteristics unique to ABC within "connection accounting" are establishing intermediate activity centers and allocating costs in a three step process, as well as using "cost drivers" corresponding to various activity centers, when allocating costs from intermediate activity centers to main activity centers.

The LRIC model was used to calculate interconnectivity fees beginning in fiscal year 2000; however, NTT East and West incurred sunk costs when this model was first applied. Moreover, NTT East and West curtailed new investment in their landline network, due to changes in the telecommunications market environment. While this resulted in an elimination of sunk costs, many fear the possibility of sunk costs reoccurring in the future. Since NTT East and West apply ABC within "connection accounting", they can implement the ABC information to conduct ABM and potentially reduce actual costs. Working with the activities used within ABC, the companies conduct a further cross-sectional reassessment of interconnection-related work, and break these down into activities that have a coordinated, mutual, linked relationship. Furthermore, by associating these newly defined activities with their respective cost drivers, the companies can root out wasteful activities and streamline other activities to enable a reduction in costs. In summary, comparing LRIC with actual expenses in a performance evaluation enables the companies to realize the gap between the LRIC target value and actual expenses.

Thus, by applying ABM that uses ABC within "connection accounting", NTT East and West can probably avoid sunk costs from occurring, when determining interconnectivity fees.

References

Bussey, B. A. (December, 1993). ABC within a service organisation, *Management Accounting*, 40–41 and 65.

Fuke, H. (2000). *Structure and Deregulation of the Information Communications Industry — A Comparative Study Between the U.S., U.K., and Japan*, Tokyo NTT (in Japanese).

Gwynne, R. and G. Ashworth (December, 1993). Implementing activity-based management at mercury communications, *Management Accounting (England)*, 34–36.

Information and Communications Council Report (2010). *Calculation of Connection Fees from Fiscal Year 2011 on the Basis of Long Run Incremental Cost Method*, September 28.

Japan Association of Management Accounting (eds.) (2000). *Managerial Accounting Dictionary*, Tokyo Chuo-Keizai (in Japanese).

Ministry of Posts (2000). *On the State of Connection Fees* (in Japanese).

Nihon Keizai Shimbun (Morning Edition) (2002). NTT plans to drop landlines entirely, April 20, p. 3; *Nihon Keizai Shimbun* (Morning edition) (September 12, 2002) NTT's investment in landlines down by 80%, p. 13 (in Japanese).

NTT West (2010). *Connection Accounting Development Procedure Manual*, (in Japanese).

NTT West (2010). *Connection Accounting Report* (In Japanese).

Raffish, N. and P. B. B. Turney (1991). Glossary of activity-based management, *Journal of Cost Management*, 5(3), 53–63.

Terrence, H., J. Thomson and P. Sharman (April, 1994). Activity-based management at AT&T, *Management Accounting*.

Turney, P. B. B. (January, 1992). Activity-Based Management, *Management Accounting*, 20–25.

PART 3

General Concepts and Techniques Applied to the Service Management

10

Omotenashi: Japanese Hospitality as the Global Standard

Nobuhiro Ikeda
Otemon Gakuin University

1 Introduction

The spirit of *omotenashi* or Japanese hospitality has a long history in Japanese culture. It is a way of providing better services in a mature society that has realized material richness. There are four criteria for a condition or environment to be deemed as *omotenashi*.

(1) The first is freedom from the pursuit of economic rationalization by eliminating waste, irregularity, and unreasonability.
(2) The second is reconsideration of the uniformity in high productivity through the use of manuals, standardization, mechanization, and automation, even though a high-mix, low-volume production pattern has created personalized consumption.
(3) The third is emphasis on a spiritual rather than a materialistic life; that is, ultimate satisfaction is achieved by shifting from possession of material goods to having actual experiences.
(4) The fourth is recovery and reconstruction of lost human relations.

This study attempts to examine the possibility of the Japanese traditional spirit of *omotenashi* as the ideal model for transactions on the basis of hospitality performed in a mature society that has realized material richness.

In this study the word "producer" means maker, distributor, and retailer who produce services, and "consumer" means the ultimate consumer or end user of services.

2   The Modern Meaning of Consumer Satisfaction in Marketing

To examine the performance of the spirit of *omotenashi* in commercial transactions, adaptability of the spirit of such transactions is needed to be investigated. Further, modern commercial transactions always require the realization of marketing that is oriented toward consumer satisfaction.

In this section, the author explains consumer satisfaction in marketing (Sec. 2.1), how consumer desires vary widely and rapidly change in modern society (Sec. 2.2), and a paradigm for consumer transactions suitable for modern consumer desires (Sec. 2.3).

2.1   *The reality of consumer satisfaction*

Marketing is usually considered an activity that seeks consumer satisfaction; however, it is actually expected to satisfy consumers to a greater degree than consumers' actual expectations. The value of goods that a consumer purchases must be larger than the price that he/she pays (value ≥ price) for those goods. In many cases, the realized level of consumer satisfaction is much higher than that expected by traditional market research containing point of sale (POS) systems. Traditional market research frequently fails to reveal the actual consumer satisfaction that the producer expects.

2.2   *Three dimensions of variations in consumer wants*

Consumer wants that vary greatly in today's modern markets differ in three dimensions.

The first dimension is variations among consumers (differences in the space dimension). Traditional market segmentation considers these differences; namely, the market is not homogeneous but heterogeneous.

The second dimension is differences in the same consumer. For example, many consumers change the watch they wear according to time, place, and occasion. They have one watch for work and another one for leisure activities.

The third dimension is the changing tastes and preferences of the same consumer. For example, consumers tend to prefer different designs, colors, and functions as time passes (differences in the time dimension).

The relationship between producers and consumers in the three dimensions is almost similar to those in the traditional Japanese expression, "*ichi-go ichi-e*". "*Ichi-go*" means one time and "*ichi-e*" means one encounter. When a man meets another man in a normal encounter, the next encounter is not always the same because people always change. Moreover, the Western culture has an almost similar expression, "You cannot step twice into the same river, for other waters are continually flowing on" (Heraclitus).

Modern consumer strategy that varies in these three dimensions is considered one-to-one marketing based on database marketing oriented toward made-to-order developments in time and space.

2.3   *The modern trade paradigm*

Trade paradigms are classified into three categories. The most primitive paradigm is a stimulus–response paradigm, the second is an exchange paradigm, and the third is a relational paradigm that has become the main trade paradigm (Shimaguchi and Ishii, 1995).

The stimulus–response paradigm states that the stronger the stimulation from the producer, the higher the consumer response toward the purchase. This paradigm, which implies that the consumer is completely passive and reacts to the one-sided operation of the producer, is no longer applicable to the modern consumer, who has better access to information and therefore actively participates in the trade.

In the exchange paradigm, both the producer and the consumer participate actively in the trade and negotiate with each other over trade conditions. The consumer is no longer passive and negotiates with the producer for better trade conditions. In the paradigm, the trade quickly concludes; therefore, the consumer and the producer cannot build a long-lasting trade relationship.

The relational paradigm, which has recently become increasingly important in trade, focuses on long-term rather than short-term interests. The producer provides consumers with the best possible solutions (customer value or customer solution) by using rich and high-level knowledge and judgment, as well as a deep insight into human psychology and behavior by listening to the voices of consumers. Examples of this include the following:

(1) *Nishiki-ya*, a *kimono* (Japanese dry goods) dealer, meets consumers' tastes by introducing other *kimono* dealers instead of getting interests for the month (Recruit Works Editorial Department, 2007, pp. 68–83).

(2) *Kaga-ya*, a Japanese-style inn, presents unexpected gifts for guests' wedding anniversaries (certainly, free of cost), or offers alternative meals for guests who do not eat raw fish (NHK, 2010).

(3) *Shiseido*, a Japanese cosmetics company, is now expanding its business in China and directs its Chinese sales representatives not to try to persuade consumers to immediately purchase their products, instead listen to consumers who discuss their skin problems (NHK, 2010).

(4) Yamato Transport Co. Ltd., while expanding its *Takkyubin* (quick delivery service) business in China, handles an expensive watermelon by making special packaging arrangements rather than refusing to deliver it because of company rules (NHK, 2010).

(5) In Sony Life Insurance's TV advertising, two men talk in a friendly manner, and we cannot distinguish between a producer and a consumer. This indicates the importance of a partnership between the consumer and the producer for better trade (TVCM, 2005).

(6) The Peninsula Tokyo records its guests' past uses (guest history) and provides guests with different and individualized services based on the guest history (adding a personal touch). This service reflects the relational paradigm by using database marketing to accomplish one-to-one marketing (Thompson, 2007).

3 Interpretation of *Omotenashi* for Consumer Satisfaction in Marketing

Omotenashi, in general, requires "form", which does not mean a manual, but is a concept that realizes ultimate consumer satisfaction in commercial trade or made-to-order consumer satisfaction based on database marketing. This section makes evident that "form" is a marketing device to cope with infinite realities.

3.1 "Form" and "ichi-go ichi-e" of omotenashi in the Japanese tea ceremony

"Form" is like a stage setting, and on a stage, various realities arise from interactions between performers and the audience. Trade realities, provided as services, are determined by interactions between producers and consumers based on the characteristics of service. The producer and the consumer of the service live in a different time and space and participate in their own stories; therefore, their stories appear once on the stage setting as the "form" and produce infinite realities (Recruit Works Editorial Department, 2007, pp. 32–47).

Although "form" does not imply uniformity, it produces more details and fineness in a category than without form. For example, in Japan, when business shirts with stripes were in vogue, they all seemed identical at first glance; however, in reality, the patterns of the stripes varied infinitely. In contrast, the Western culture has many categories but fewer variations within each category. This signifies that the details and fineness in Japan satisfy the taste of each consumer.

3.2   *Story returns to power; beyond the limit of the anti-novel economy*

Although economic rationality seeks results as efficiently as possible, the world of *omotenashi* weighs into the process. Different from many practical business books, the manner in which we read stories and novels is similar to traveling, where we involve ourselves in the process rather than the result (Ikeda, 2003).

Each producer and consumer lives his/her own story; therefore, both have different processes regardless of whether the results are the same or different. This is the spirit of *ichi-go ichi-e*.

Stories ask readers to read between the lines, where non-verbal content is contained, which vary infinitely for the author and the reader; that is, non-verbal content differs among those concerned with the business transaction.

The spirit of *"ichi-go ichi-e"* is the same as that of one-to-one marketing because of its different approach to each individual consumer.

3.3   *Differences between a manual and "form"*

While a manual guarantees a minimum quality of services by standardizing operations, "form" represents the criteria for measuring the differences between the producer and the consumer. The differences between the producer and the consumer as related to criteria give them imaginative adaptability of services that has no upper limit.

A manual represents instructions to employees who provide a service to consumers, where no training is needed for the latter who receive the service. On the other hand, "form" also demands training the consumer, including adequate experience, knowledge, intelligence, and insight. This presents the relationship between the producer and the consumer: the consumer educates the producer and vice versa, a process related to training in *omotenashi*, which is explained later.

4   Relationship between *Omotenashi* and Hospitality

In Japan, the word *omotenashi* is inequivalent to its English translation "hospitality". In this section, the differences between these two words are clarified.

There are three types of literature referring to *omotenashi* and hospitality.

(A)   *Omotenashi* and hospitality have the same meaning (Hayashida, 2006; Yamakami, 2008).

(B)   There is no reference to the differences between *omotenashi* and hospitality (Kotler *et al.*, 2002; Nakamura and Yamaguchi, 2002; Hosoi, 2006, 2010; Orido, 2010).

(C)   There are references to the differences between *omotenashi* and hospitality (Thompson, 2007; Recruit Works Editorial Department, 2007).

Almost all literature belongs to A and B. In this study, C is useful only for revealing the differences between *omotenashi* and hospitality.

4.1   *"Omotenashi" is the ultimate spirit of hospitality*

At the Peninsula Tokyo, guests experience the hotel's spirit of hospitality as the sum of services provided or as each service appears to them. Although the guests do not count the services, they can feel the hospitality as part of the entire experience. Each service is a means or a concrete operation (for the guest, a concrete experience) to bring to reality the spirit of hospitality (Thompson, 2007, p. 148).

The phrase "personal touch" is used by the Peninsula Tokyo, and it reflects the actual services or operations that are personalized for each guest. This personal touch represents *omotenashi* at the Peninsula Tokyo, where the ultimate means is to achieve the success of traditional Japanese services *omotenashi* in the Western culture (Thompson, 2007, pp. 153–154).

4.2   *Omotenashi in the modern economy*

The consumer, the receiver of *omotenashi*, could be called a "prosumer" in the modern economy. "Prosumer", a marketing word, means a consumer who develops the merchandise with the producer (Recruit Works Editorial Department, 2007, pp. 136–137).

In addition, marketing traditionally has four means to approach consumers for the purpose of purchasing products. One approach is called "promotion", an activity in which a producer provides information about merchandise to consumers. Today, we use "communication" instead of "promotion" that implies the relationship between consumers and producers varies in the relational paradigm.

In service marketing, the producer and the consumer cooperatively produce higher value merchandise. This can be seen through *"omotenashi"* in the Japanese tea ceremony, where the host effortlessly exchanges places with the guest. The host educates the guest and vice versa (Recruit Works Editorial Department, 2007, pp. 134–135). This interaction is not limited to the ceremony. In a mature economy, consumers have sufficient information as producers, the roles of consumers and producers are constantly being replaced, time and again.

The frequent replacement of the host (producer) and the guest (consumer) brings a clear change to personal management. In *"omotenashi"*, traditional personal management fails to work because the market — the set of consumers — varies frequently, as mentioned earlier. As a result, decision-making takes a long time and does not keep up with market movements. To solve this problem, a non-managerial organization is suitable as hospitality requires management at the top level and *omotenashi* requires the employee to make autonomous and quick decisions at the operational level of service. (Recruit Works Editorial Department, 2007, pp. 120–121).

Although decision-making in *omotenashi* occasionally requires extra expenses and incurs losses in the short term, the relational paradigm captures the loyalty of guests that is in the best interest of the producer and consumer satisfaction in the long term.

5   Learning and Teaching *Omotenashi*

This section examines whether the Japanese traditional spirit of *omotenashi* can be introduced to other countries. The main issue is whether others can be trained and educated in *omotenashi*.

5.1   *Master and pupil relation and "kaban-mochi"*

It is necessary for a producer to sometimes be the master and sometimes be the pupil, and to learn and teach both verbal and non-verbal information, skills, and techniques.

In Japan, people have the traditional habit of teaching and learning non-verbal information by observing and following every move that the master makes. The master, at certain instances, teaches pupils practical know-how through words; however, the ability to "*sassuru*" (Japanese verb) or "read the air" is particularly important for the pupil. On occasions, the pupil follows the master everywhere and observes what happens in the business. This practice is called "*kaban-mochi*", where "*kaban*" means master's briefcase and "*mochi*" means the bringer. The pupil moves like the master's shadow.

Explaining "*sassuru*" and "read the air" in English is difficult. Some Japanese–English dictionaries explain "*sassuru*" as "guess", "suppose", "presume", "assume", and "imagine". Other dictionaries explain that "*sassuru*" is to know what to say and what to do without any verbal explanation. In the Western world, the verbs "guess", "suppose", "presume", "assume", and "imagine" require facts or data to understand what to say and what to do.

The Japanese may receive and distinguish among very subtle signs. In the example of business shirts with stripes given earlier, the reaction of others is slower than usual by 0.1 second because these products have many variations with subtle differences. This reaction reflects the ability to find very small signs, differences, and changes.

In Japanese culture, people do not express their opinions clearly but change their opinions slightly according to subtle changes in others. What to do and what to say depend on others and the environment or the atmosphere. Although, in the Western culture, this traditional aspect of Japanese culture is absent, carrying out the spirit of *omotenashi* is useful and important even in the Western society.

5.2 *Kaizen*

The Japanese managerial word "*kaizen*" means that there is no limit to improving operations as there is always much room for improvement. *Omotenashi* is always imperfect because the producer must improvise at times even though it perfectly prepares all things in advance (Recruit Works Editorial Department, 2007, pp. 125–130). The producer must take steps to manage every situation that occurs in "*ichi-go ichi-e*"; thus, the consumer quickly and dramatically varies in three dimensions. Once *omotenashi* is successful, we may continue to provide the same *omotenashi*, but doing so is dangerous because the roles of both the producer and the customer are changing constantly.

The word *"kaizen"* was first used in factory management and was gradually adopted by management in all fields. Today, the word is used not only for products but also for services in commercial transactions. Since consumers always change their tastes and lifestyles, *"kaizen"* provides for the possibility of evolving and spreading the spirit of *omotenashi*.

6   Conclusion

Omotenashi is an advanced sprit of hospitality in the Western culture, a rather useful model in an ever-changing market and in a mature society, and provides much insight into hospitality.

Especially, a mature society requires commercial trade to show the spirit of *omotenashi*, where relational paradigm is dominated. Further, *"ichi-go ichi-e"* of the producer and the consumer in *omotenashi* has high affinity with one-to-one marketing. In addition, the "form" of *omotenashi* is a marketing device that produces made-to-order satisfaction and is completely different from a manual.

The question of whether *omotenashi* is adaptable to other countries is answerable with the original Japanese word *"kaizen"*. The master and pupil relationship and *"kaizen"* demand that the producer and the consumer engage in a long-term learning relationship, that is, in a relational paradigm. A producer and a consumer must constantly learn from each other to obtain the required experience, knowledge, intelligence, and insight.

References

Hayashida, M. (2006). *Text of Hospitality, Heartfelt Omotenashi for Impressing the Guest*, Tokyo: Asa Publisher (in Japanese).

Hosoi, M. (2006). *Manner of Kaga-Ya, First-Rate Omotenashi*, Tokyo: PHP (in Japanese).

Hosoi, M. (2010). *Heart of Kaga-Ya, Human-Oriented Management*, Tokyo: PHP (in Japanese).

Ikeda, N. (2003). Haruki Murakami as a market barometer: Beyond the limit of the anti-novel economy, *HUE Journal of Economics and Business*, 26(2), 25–42 (in Japanese).

Kotler, P., J. T. Bowen and J. C. Makens. (2002). *Marketing for Hospitality and Tourism*, 3rd ed., Upper Saddle River, NJ: Prentice Hall (translated by Hayashi, S. (2003). Pearson Education Japan).

Nakamura, K. and Y. Yamaguchi (2002). *Hospitality Management: Theory and Case Study to Improve Competitive Power and Service*, Tokyo: Seisansei Publisher (in Japanese).

NHK, (2010). Get the business chance in the world with Omotenashi, *Close Up Gendai (TV Program)* 26 July, Tokyo: NHK (in Japanese).

Orido, H. (2010). *Challenge of Restaurant and Hotel–Hospitality Management*, Tokyo: Tamagawa University Publication (in Japanese).

Recruit Works Editorial Department (2007). *The Origin of Omotenashi: The Essence of Service in Japanese Tradition*, Tokyo: Eichi Publication (in Japanese).

Shimaguchi, M. and J. Ishii (1995). *Modern Marketing*, New Edition, Tokyo: Yuhikaku (in Japanese).

Sony Life Insurance Co. Ltd., (2005). TVCM, Tokyo, Sony Life Insurance Co. Ltd.

Thompson, M. (2007). *The Spirit of Hospitality: Learning from the Japanese Experience*, Tokyo: Shoudensha (in Japanese).

Yamakami, T. (2008). *Evolution of the Spirit of Omotenashi for Creating the Omotenashi Culture*, Kyoto: Houritsu-Bunka-Sha (in Japanese).

11

The Service Level Agreements at Japanese Companies and Its Expansion

Tomoaki Sonoda
Keio University

1 Introduction

Although the service industry has been developing and expanding recently, the main research target of management accounting is the manufacturing industry. There has been management accounting research about the service industry, for example, Okamoto (1993), Aoki (1999, 2000), and Sonoda (2006).

On the other hand, there are many different kinds of companies in the service industry, with a variety of characteristics. One service company has certain unique characteristics, and another has different features. It makes it difficult to study the management of the service industry overall.

This chapter classifies the service industry in four categories using two axes:

(1) The level of standardization of services,
(2) The number of customers (mass customers or specific customers).

This chapter focuses on the fourth service-industry domain in order to handle these issues. Data processing companies and shared services companies are located in the fourth domain. Some of these companies in Japan intend to use Service Level Agreements (SLAs) that manage service quality. These companies provide standardized services to a few particular customers.

This chapter discusses SLAs and their expansion, especially the adoption of service level manifestos in the rail industry and mail industry that provide standardized services to mass customers (the first domain).

2 Difficulty in Separating the Service Industry and the Manufacturing Industry

2.1 *Service activities in the manufacturing industry*

Beyond service activities provided by service companies, there are several service activities in manufacturing companies, such as supporting activities in factories, sales, after-services, administration activities, etc. After-services are essential services in manufacturing companies to repair and replace defective products. On the other hand, because of the characteristic of simultaneity of delivery and consumption, service companies do not repair or replace their services after they have delivered the services.

Manufacturing companies sometimes provide services to other companies. Some manufacturing companies lease the machines and cars they produce. Food companies often have restaurant divisions. Recently, accounting and payroll departments are using shared services and outsourcing. Shared services are a management method for administrative functions from the viewpoint of corporate group management, which (1) centralize administrative functions of the parent company and group companies to the shared services center (SSC), (2) reexamine functions, and (3) standardize functions (Sonoda, 2007). Shared services centers that are established in a manufacturing company generally provide their services to group companies.

2.2 *Similarity of manufacturing industry characteristics to the service industry*

Some parts of the service industry have the same characteristics as the manufacturing industry. Generally speaking, the characteristics of services are (1) intangible and (2) simultaneously delivered and consumed. But there are some cases that differ from these general characteristics of service-industry companies. Restaurants serve meals and fish; these are tangible. Companies lend machines or equipments, which are tangible, through leasing companies. They use them for a specific period, and this means leased machines do not have the characteristic of simultaneous delivery and consumption. Shared services centers deliver tangibles that are hard-copy data, such as financial statements and books, to their clients.

Some service companies have inventories or materials. Examples of companies that have inventories are retailers such as supermarkets and department stores. Ten Allied, which runs Teng, a chain of Japanese-style pubs, accounts for semi-products on its balance sheet. Ten Allied calculates production costs using process costing, and material costs are 73.5%[1] of total production costs (FY 2009). Ten Allied also has a central kitchen that serves as a logistics hub and processing plant. Hakuyosya, a cleaning company, has factories such as its Tamagawa factory.

Imperial Hotel deducts not only sales and administrative costs but also material costs, and material costs are 23.5% of sales (FY 2009). The ratio of tangibles (after deducting depreciation) on total assets of All Nippon Airways is 63.1%. The same ratio for Imperial Hotel and East Japan Railway Company are 55.6% and 83.4%. These tangible ratio numbers mean that airlines, hotels, and railways are service industry companies that have features of the apparatus industry.

2.3 *Adoption of management accounting in the service industry*

Management accounting has developed mainly to solve the problems of manufacturing companies, and there has been little research to adapt management accounting to the service industry in Japan. Aoki (1999) shows the following four reasons why management accounting has not done research on service companies: (1) a good portion of service businesses are small businesses; (2) sales are more important than costs; (3) the outputs of service companies are not standardized; (4) management accounting does not differ between manufacturing and services companies.

Even in light of these reasons, there are very few management accounting tools that are difficult to adapt to the service industry. Service companies can use CVP analysis, divisional accounting, and budgeting the same as manufacturing companies. Variable costing and capital budgeting are helpful for airlines, hotels, and railways, which have a large amount of capital investment and fixed costs. Okada (2010) examines target costing for service companies.

Kirin Brewery Company additionally participated in cooperative distribution in Hokkaido within Sapporo Breweries, Takara Shuzo, and Sanwa Shurui. Sonoda (2010) explains the validity of this decision-making by Kirin through differential analysis. Sonoda (2006) shows that four shared services companies adopted a balanced scorecard (BSC) and presents the

---

[1]The numbers in this section are drawn from annual reports.

perspective of the parent company, which is the fifth perspective of the BSC as a practical finding.

3   Definition of the Service Industry and Its Classification

3.1   *Definition of the service industry*

There are many service companies in the intermediate regions between the manufacturing and service industries. It is difficult to define the service industry as distinct from the manufacturing industry because the majority of service companies have characteristics of manufacturing companies. This chapter defines the service industry not from the viewpoint of intangibility and simultaneity of delivery and consumption, but rather from the viewpoint of cost construction, which is a management accounting perspective: "The service industry has unique cost distinctions. Their main additional inputs *vis-à-vis* outputs are not materials; the main additional inputs of the service industry are labor activities, and then their main incremental costs are labor costs".

This definition requires four notes. First, there are many service companies in the intermediate regions. For example, incremental costs of restaurants are not only labor costs but also material costs. Second, for apparatus industries such as hotels, depreciation expenses are the main cost factors, but they are not additional costs because they are fixed costs. Third, if service companies pay labor costs as fixed monthly salaries, when employees work to provide services without overtime work, there are no additional costs. Fourth, if we change the word *industry* to *activities* in the above definition, this definition can be adopted to the internal services of the manufacturing industry.

3.2   *Classification of the service industry*

Figure 1 shows four types of service companies. This chapter divides the service industry into four categories using two axes: (1) the level of standardization of services, and (2) the number of customers (mass customers or specific customers).

The first domain is service companies that provide standardized services to mass customers. Post offices, railways, airlines, and home delivery services belong to the first domain. Shared services companies and the data-processing companies provide standardized services, but they deliver their services to specific customers under contract. So, these service companies are located in the fourth domain.

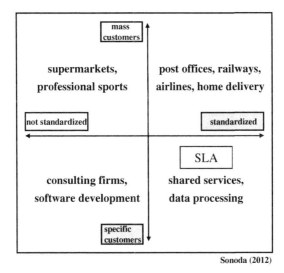

Sonoda (2012)

Fig. 1.   Four types of service companies.

Information companies that develop software belong to the third domain because the software developed is not standardized but customized. Consulting firms also belong to the third domain. On the other hand, supermarkets and professional sports belong to the second domain because they deliver their services to mass customers even though they do not provide standardized services like third-domain service companies.

4   Why Is Service Quality Important?

4.1   *Influence of the accounting characteristics of services on service quality*

First, because of the definition of the service industry, the main additional costs are labor costs. Therefore, employees' work and activities significantly influence the quality of services. It means that service quality will vary widely. This point is different from manufacturing companies with factories that have a high degree of automation.

Second, there are correlative relationships between the costs and quality of services because the main additional costs are labor costs. When companies reduce the input of labor power for cost reduction, the quality of services accordingly may fall. If companies want to improve the quality of services, companies should increase labor power, and then costs will go up. Sonoda (2006) states that the main agenda for a shared services center is to successfully manage this correlative relationship of cost and quality.

4.2 Influence of the quality of services on profitability

Service companies should expend additional costs because of low service quality, for example, food poisoning in restaurants. Since services generally have the characteristic of simultaneous delivery and consumption, consumers may buy the same services many times. However, bad-quality services lead to a decrease in repeat purchases, and then profitability falls. These future decreases in repeat buyers are construed as opportunity costs. On the other hand, replacement and repair costs of faulty products are not generally incurred by service companies.

4.3 Deterioration of service level caused by clients

Clients sometimes have negative effects on the level of services they receive. Personnel management outsourcers provide payroll services after they receive data about overtime work and absences of employees from client companies. If these data contain errors, outsourcers will incorrectly calculate paychecks. It is difficult for outsourcers to take corrective action because client companies have caused these problems.

5 Service Level Agreements

5.1 What are service level agreements?

Service Level Agreements (SLAs) are contractual documents or their attachments that define the services provided, service prices, quality of services, and penalty for failure in quality (Sonoda, 2006). SLAs have developed as a tool to manage IT outsourcers. If services have gaps between targets and performance levels, low service levels will be improved to target levels. Outsourcers sometimes will pay a penalty and sometimes will change contractual prices.

5.2 Management process using SLAs

Figure 2 shows the management process using SLAs for payroll services. SLAs stipulate an error ratio as a measure of service quality and set a

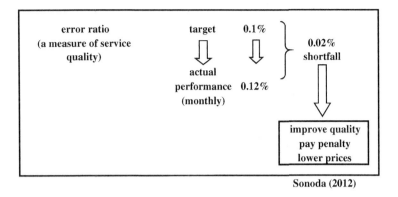

Sonoda (2012)

Fig. 2.   Management process using a SLA for payroll services.

target of 0.1% per month. If the actual error ratio is 0.12%, the actual performance level falls short of the target by 0.02 percentage points. The outsourcer analyzes the gaps between the target and the performance level, and takes action to reduce the error ratio. If SLAs include a penalty, the outsourcer pays it to the company that entrusts it with the payroll. If the error ratio does not improve, prices may go down, or the client company may ask to lower the prices or change the outsourcer.

5.3   *Service companies that can use SLAs*

There are three prerequisites to using SLAs, because SLAs are contractual documents or their attachments:

(1) Provide services continuously,
(2) Provide services to specific customers,
(3) Services provided are standardized by a few measurements.

Data processing companies and shared services companies meet these three requirements because they provide standardized services continuously to specific customers with agreements. SLAs are effective for these service companies, which are placed in the fourth domain in Fig. 1.

5.4   *Nonfinancial targets in SLAs*

Targets of service are stipulated in SLAs by using nonfinancial indexes, for example, error ratios for payroll. Main performance indexes for sports are the number of victories, winning percentage, and the number of spectators (Sonoda and Yokota, 2010). SLAs need to have adequate indexes to manage the quality of services.

There are three types of nonfinancial indexes: (1) physical indexes, (2) rates, and (3) ranks (Sonoda, 1999). SLAs can use these typical nonfinancial indexes: on-time delivery ratios, error ratios, and time taken to adjust errors. When a SLA uses a ratio of errors as a quality index and the actual ratio is beyond the target, the outsourcer breaks down the error ratio to each employee and activity, analyzes the factors for errors, and improves the level of service.

6 Expansion of SLAs

6.1 *Expansion of SLAs within the third domain*

SLAs are basically a management tool by which client companies manage outsourcers' level of services. Even though shared services companies provide their services mostly to group companies, they are a kind of outsourcer. But some shared services companies in Japan use or tend to use SLAs to manage their own activities. One of the main missions of shared services companies is remediation of their quality of services. They expect that employees will be more concerned about quality of services by showing them SLA targets. Advanced quality of services will facilitate group companies to entrust their work to shared services companies. This situation indicates that service companies can adopt SLAs to manage their own quality of services, even though, in general, client companies use SLAs to manage service companies as outsourcers.

6.2 *The case of NTT business associe*

NTT Business Associe (NTT-BA) is a shared services company for the NTT group. One section of its accounting division checks contractual documents that one of the group companies has made. NTT-BA signs with this group company, and its agreements contain some points that have characteristics of SLAs. Because the contractual documents that NTT-BA checks are in a standardized format, these checking activities are easy to manage by agreements. Their agreements stipulate lead times to check contractual documents within three business days.

Although their agreements do not stipulate it, error ratios depending on the client company (the client company writes "incorrect" on the documents) should be under 20%. If a client company makes errors over 20%, prices may be adjusted upward when they renew their agreements because NTT-BA measures times with a stopwatch to require an additional 30 minutes depending on each client's error (Sonoda, 2011).

7 Service Level Manifestos

This chapter suggests a new concept of service level manifestos as a second expansion of SLAs. Service companies that belong to the first domain in Fig. 1 and provide standardized services can use service level manifestos, even though they serve mass customers. Typical companies in the first domain are post offices, railways, airlines, and home delivery services. If they adopt service level manifestos, they promise a level of services to customers and manage their own level of services. Service level manifestos are not a tool of contracts, but a tool to gain trust from mass consumers through service companies' fulfillment to meet targets. Service level manifestos are an expansion of SLAs from the fourth domain to the first domain (Fig. 3).

Since service companies placed in the first domain provide standardized services to mass customers, they can easily make indexes to measure the quality of services. However, their customers are not specific but mass, so they cannot make an SLA with each customer. Alternatively,

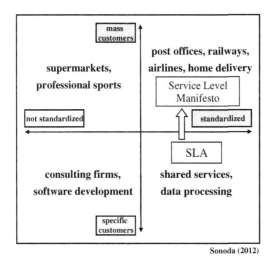

Sonoda (2012)

Fig. 3.   Service-level manifesto.

service companies disclose service level manifestos to promise their level of service to mass customers for the purpose of winning the confidence of customers. This concept is analogous to the expansion of SLAs in the fourth domain because service companies make indexes of their own service levels on their own. Service level manifestos need to establish targets of service quality and to disclose them in advance, aside from disclosing actual quality performance levels. It is also important to analyze gaps between targets and performance levels in order to improve service levels.

Many Japanese service companies bring in practical operations similar to service level manifestos. All Nippon Airways discloses safety and flight data on its website and publishes the *ANA Group Safety Report* under the Civil Aeronautics Act. Its flight data shows operational data (flight cancellations and services), turn-back rates, diversion rates, and on-time departure rates. East Japan Railway Company states in its delay and cancellation policy, "If limited express or express trains are delayed more than two hours, charges will be fully refunded" (www.jreast.co.jp/e/ticket/accidents.html). This statement is similar to penalty covenants of SLAs. Home delivery companies in Japan have a services menu in which customers can choose the day when their packages will arrive. These analogies predicate that possible candidates for indexes of service level manifestos are indexes related to delivery times.

8 Conclusion

This chapter classifies the service industry in four categories using two axes:

(1) The level of standardization of the services,
(2) The number of customers (mass customers or specific customers).

Shared services companies and data processing companies in the fourth domain in Fig. 1 can use SLAs. This chapter names SLAs that are adopted by service companies in the first domain as service level manifestos. Post offices, railways, airlines, and home delivery companies that provide standardized services to mass customers can use service level manifestos to promise their level of services to consumers and win their confidence. Moreover, they can improve their level of services by analyzing differences between targets and actual performance. Some service companies placed in the first domain have practices similar to service level manifestos, but it is uncertain whether they make and disclose targets preliminarily and how they improve their level of services on the basis of actual performance.

Service companies in the third domain may probably use SLAs because their clients are specific and they sign contracts with them. But their services are normally not both continuous and standardized, so it may be difficult to use intensive indexes such as error ratios. Service companies in the second domain cannot adopt SLAs. They need to use other tools to manage their level of services, for example, customer satisfaction surveys.

References

Aoki, A. (1999). Basic framework of management accounting in the service industry, *Mita Business Review*, 42(4), 133–159 (in Japanese).

Aoki, A. (2000). Examination of ordinarily-used management accounting methods in the service industry, *Mita Business Review*, 43(2), 89–108 (in Japanese).

Okada, Y. (2010). A key roll of service target costing for SSME research & education in Japan, *KAIKEI*, 177(1), 63–78 (in Japanese).

Okamoto, K. ed. (1993). *Management Accounting for Software and Services*, Tokyo: Chuo-keizaisya (in Japanese).

Sonoda, T. (1999). Strategic management accounting and nonfinancial measures, *Mita Business Review*, 41(6), 103–121 (in Japanese).

Sonoda, T. (2006). *Management Accounting for Shared Services*, Tokyo: Chuo-keizaisya (in Japanese).

Sonoda, T. (2007). Characteristics of Japanese shared service centers, in Y. Monden *et al.* (eds.), *Japanese Management Accounting Today*, Singapore: World Scientific Publishing.

Sonoda, T. (2010). Shared services between several business groups: Cooperative distribution of alcoholic companies in Hokkaido area, *The Journal of Cost Accounting Research*, 34(2), 139–149 (in Japanese).

Sonoda, T. (2011). The use of service level agreement and its expansion: The proposal of service level manifesto, *Mita Business Review*, 53(6), 43–53 (in Japanese).

Sonoda, T. (2012). Management of service quality using service level agreement, *KAIKEI*, 181(1), 60–71 (in Japanese).

Sonoda, T. and Yokota, E. (2010). *An Introduction to Cost and Management Accounting*, Tokyo: Chuo-keizaisya (in Japanese).

12

Application of Information and Communication Technology to the Service Industry — Focus on Business Process Network

Yoshiyuki Nagasaka
Konan University

Gunyung Lee
Niigata University

1   Introduction

The term "business model" came to be used in various scenarios after a business model was patented in 1998 in the United States. Even in the service industry, superior business models have been developed and maintained. In Japan, various activities are undertaken, such as creating new markets, developing cost competitiveness through efficient processes, and creating value through differentiation.

The recent environmental change has had a big influence on the management of enterprises. From the viewpoint of the competitive environment, competition among individual firms has already changed to competition among value chains or company alliances. In order to take competitive advantage of this environmental change, it is necessary to construct a business process network (BPN) among allied companies to efficiently run multiple processes and deal with problems in a real time manner. BPN is considered as a business model in a broad sense.

In this chapter, we summarize the situation of the representative ICT applications in the service industry of Japan and consider each type of business model. Second, we discuss the significance and the effects of BPN with some examples from the service industry.

2 Structure and Type of Business Model in the Service Industry

Literally, the word "services" comes from "serve", which means to work for another with hospitality. The service industry in Japan is considered unique in its approach to providing service. It is different from the service industry in other countries. Therefore, it is necessary to compare the productivity of the Japanese service industry with that of other countries. For example, in the food service industry in Japan, a moist hand towel and a glass of water are served free in restaurants. Chairs are positioned for customers to wait if the restaurant is crowded. This is rare abroad.

Barbers in Japan offer not only haircuts but also hair washes, shaves, and massages. Abroad, barbers are only for hair cutting.

Long lines of customers form at the cash register in overseas supermarkets and convenience stores because it takes time to pay. In Japan, however, the staff and the number of salesclerks at the cash register can be increased flexibly to reduce customers' waiting time. At gas stations in Japan, a shop clerk cleans the ashtray and the windows of the car. Japanese taxi drivers open and close the door for customers. When I enter a bank in Japan, a guide talks to me and assists me in filling in forms. Thus, the Japanese service industry provides excellent, considerate hospitality.

However, there may be some problems with service in Japan in fields such as finance (banks and insurance), the IT industry, medical care, health care, and housing and real estate. For example, the housing loan conditions offered by banks in Japan are rigorous. The waiting time is long in hospitals in Japan, and more medicine than necessary may be prescribed. Real estate brokers in Japan charge a fee to both the seller and the buyer.

Most Japanese worry about objects and request careful service, and do not mind too much of it.

2.1 *The productivity of service industries*

Looy *et al.* (2004) have defined services as immaterial nature because of process, simultaneous nature of manufacture and consumption, extinction nature of stock, and heterogeneity depending on each person. Shimomura *et al.* (2009) have defined service as "the action that causes a required change of state for the customer by the provider of service with some money". According to these definitions, the productivity of the service industry can be measured using specific methods that are different from those used for the manufacturing industry (Naito, 2010).

Table 1.   A comparison of labor productivity (1995–2003).

Type of industry	USA	UK	Germany	Japan
Manufacturing industry	3.3%	2.0%	1.7%	4.1%
Service industry	2.3%	1.3%	0.9%	0.8%

Source: Ministry of Economy, Trade and Industry, 2007 (Naito, 2010, p. 13).

Generally, productivity is expressed by the value of the produced object divided by the resources spent on its production. In the manufacturing industry, the formula for this is productivity = product/labor force committed (person, thing, and money). The following formula has been proposed by the Ministry of Economy, Trade and Industry of Japan to measure the productivity of the service industry:

The productivity of the service industry = (accretion of added value + creation of new business)/improvement of efficiency.   (1)

A comparison of labor productivity is shown in Table 1. The productivity of the manufacturing industry in Japan is higher than it is in other countries, but that of the service industry in Japan is lower. For example, lower numbers of salesclerks are placed in supermarkets in the United States, and there is much more staff in Japan for the same sales amount. This means that labor productivity is lower in Japan.

Do Japanese supermarkets provide excessive service? For better numerical evaluation, should Japanese consumers not demand surplus services? However, this question is hardly logical. We should come up with ways to increase productivity while maintaining the quality of hospitality and customer satisfaction. In other words, it is important to raise efficiency through process improvement and increase value-addition to improve the productivity of the service industry.

2.2   *Structure of business model*

there are various definitions of the business model. The broadest definition includes three fields: the business paradigm, the business system (business process), and the business architecture. On the other hand, in a narrow sense, the business model is described as a business theory (or business concept), a business system (or a conceptual model, a theoretic

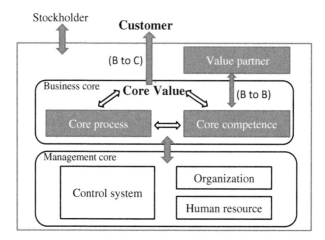

Fig. 1.　Constitution of business model.

model, or a practical model), and a business practice (or business method) (Ishikawa, 2001). Furthermore, a business model is not an action plan, an improvement plan, a behavior pattern, a set of tactics, or a strategy. The business model is indicated as a system that can create unknown values (Magretta, 2002).

These indications are common where business model refers to a basic framework of the business to create customers. Figure 1 shows a schematic constitution of the business model (Teramoto and Iwasaki, 2000).

Core value in Fig. 1 refers to customer value. In other words, in the business model, it should be clear which customer, product, or service is advantageous by considering stakeholders such as customers, stockholders, employees, and so on. Therefore, the three elements of core competence, core process, and value partner are important. Core competence is embodied in core business processes. The management system is also necessary. In addition, the suitable organization and placement of core persons are important.

On the other hand, the business model patent is important as a means to protect the business model from other companies. The patent object was originally limited to the structure but has now been extended to include software and business model. However, not all business models are accepted for patents. As for the patent, the object should include "a technical idea using natural law". (1) novelty, (2) newness, and (3) progressiveness are necessary. The business model patent is a patent of a business model with inventiveness, for eventual use of the ICT (Honjo, 1999).

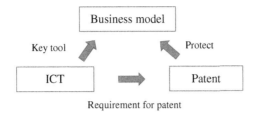

Fig. 2.   Business model, ICT, and patent.

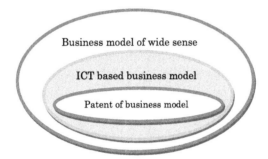

Fig. 3.   Field of business model.

A typical example of the business model patent is "the sales system of the airline ticket" in the U.S.. It is a new business technique called the name-your-price auction. Newness was accepted through internet usage.

The relationships among business model, ICT, and patent are shown in Fig. 2. When a company is going to protect its business model through a patent, patent acquisition requirements should be considered in the initial stage of business model construction. In other words, it is important to clarify the requirements/specifications of the ICT as unique and original ideas for a business model patent (Cho, 2002). "The business model constructed based on ICT", including the strict business model that can be protected by a patent, is shown in Fig. 3. In this chapter, we focus on business models based on ICT for the service industry.

It is important to consider the three layers shown in Fig. 4 in order to plan, develop, and implement a business model. The relationships between each layer are expressed as follows:

In the business model layer, a manager and a businessperson in charge create a design of the business model and a plan, and set goals. In this layer, executive officers create a design of the business model and set the

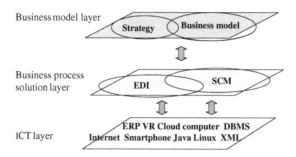

Fig. 4.   Three layers to develop a business model.

goal. In the business process solution layer, the middle manager and staff design a solution for the business model and carry it out. In the ICT layer, an IT engineer and vendor develop elemental technology, which is a system and software for the solution. Three kinds of embodiment methods are considered as follows:

(1) A bottom-up type: New processes and solutions are proposed from each technique of the ICT. These are incorporated in a business model.
(2) A top-down type: First, a business model is designed. Then, new processes and solution are selected, considering ICT based on the strategy.
(3) A middle-spread type: The business model is planned based on a solution, and a relationship with ICT is designed.

Business model construction is enabled from each position or viewpoint.

2.3   A typical example and classification of the business model

There are several types of management strategies for business models, such as the consolidation, diversification, and defensive strategies (David, 1999). However, the constitution of the business model is considered as shown in Fig. 1, and does not depend on the type of strategy. Additionally, there are several types of business model, such as B-to-C (company/customers), B-to-B (company/companies), and In-house (only in the company).

In this chapter, as shown in Table 2, the type of business model in the service industry is classified according to purpose and effect, such as marketing model (for customer exploitation and/or sustentation), added-value model (high quality and/or customer benefit), and efficiency model (cost reduction, optimized delivery, and good solution for environmental problems).

Table 2.   Types of business models in the service industry.

	Model	Summary	ICT application
1	Marketing model	Excellent for developing and retaining customers	Point card, electronic coupon, DS zone, IC tag
2	Value-added model	Prominent benefits for customers by high quality and/or unique processes	Traceability, control of freshness, QR code
3	Efficient model	Drastic improvement of cost, delivery, and environmental problems	POS, IC card electronic money, vending machine, handy terminal

(1) Marketing model

It is very important for the service industry to create new customers and increase the number of repeat (regular) customers. For example, in department stores in Japan, VIP customers (dossers) account for 80% of sales. Direct mails are sent to VIP customers about special exhibitions, and services are provided to VIP customers by off-premise sales departments.

Customer exploitation also takes place through traditional advertising methods such as magazine and newspaper advertisements and CM in TV broadcasting. Distributing small advertising catalogs between pocket tissues in the street is a unique method in Japan to get passers-by to view these catalogs. Unique point services have become popular in Japan to increase the number of repeat customers.

(2) A value-added model

The creation of value-added improvement and/or new businesses is considered to increase the outcome of Equation (1) on productivity in the service industry. It is important to offer high-quality service. Reliability and safety are required to protect the faith of the customer. In addition, delivering in short lead times or just in time makes customers happy. This can create a good feeling that affects the global environment positively. Since diversity in management can support individual customer needs, the need for variety is substantial.

For example, it is possible to choose a time as well as a date for home delivery in Japan. Cool courier services for refrigerated products and golf club courier services are also popular. Through these services, the added value of the home delivery service has improved.

(3) An efficiency model

An improvement in efficiency and cost reduction can reduce the denominator in Equation (1) and benefit productivity in the service industry. Each process should be improved to reduce effort, and automatic machines should be installed. Alternatively, self-service by customers can reduce costs.

There are more than one million vending machines in Japan, which creates a market of more than 2 trillion yen. The automatic vending machine is a convenient retail shop at which we can buy cold or hot drinks anytime we want. There are vending machines at which we can purchase with electronic money such as "wallet mobile phones" and IC cards. Withdrawal of the proceeds of sales of the vending machine and the supplying of change requires manual labor. IC cards can reduce this need. In addition, purchase data can be saved and an analysis of the relationship between marketable goods and constituency can be conducted. Some vending machines require a deposit of 10 yen for a paper cup. This amount is refunded when the paper cup is returned to the vending machine. This is unique from the perspective of environmental problems.

The 100-yen (one coin) shop is popular in Japan. A variety of products varying in cost ratio can be purchased with one coin. That is, the price of all items is the same. At stores like these, time spent at the cash register can be reduced by using price cards.

Internet stationery site, "ASKUL", which is limited to corporate transactions, increases sales through small orders and quick delivery services, such as delivery on the next day ("ASU" means "tomorrow" and "KUL" means "come" in Japanese). One can order even a ballpoint pen or an eraser. This model has been a success in Japan owing to its speed.

3   ICT Application in the Japanese Service Industry Business Model

3.1   *Examples of surface transport or the train service industry*

The Japanese railway network is substantial. It is the means of transportation for many people in urban areas. Service is provided according to the train timetable, and the quality of this service is competitive. The PTC (Programmed Traffic Control) system is an integrated system that is used to manage centralized traffic control (CTC), a driving rearranging system, and a traveler guidance system collectively. It was introduced mainly for efficiency and passenger service improvement in train scheduling management on rapid-transit railway lines such as the high-density driving railroad section or the Shinkansen (super express) of the metropolis. These lines provide ordinary services, according to a diagram.

Customers who are EXPRESS members of Shinkansen are offered facilities such as credit card payment and net reservation (a member can change their reservations repeatedly before taking a train). The customer can pass a wicket without tickets, using the EX-IC service. This helps reduce congestion at the counter (through the manual sale of tickets) and labor and facilitates train timetable adjustment.

On the train service in urban areas and subways, the IC cards shown in Fig. 5 are widely used. IC card are provided by companies such as ICOCA, PiTaPa, Suica, TOICA, PASPY, and SUGOCA in each railway network and are mutually available in each area. The ticket inspector does not need to make contact, and the construction of the flow database is enabled. A new, supplementary service sends an e-mail to the parent when a child passes the wicket. Shopping is possible with this IC card at more than 100,000 stores in stations and towns.

3.2 *Examples of retail and distribution business*

The introduction of the POS is common in major supermarkets and convenience stores. This affects the efficiency of the cash register, the fixed-quantity ordering system, the grasp of a sale line, and slow-moving items and products. The IC tag attached to the cart is utilized to analyze customer actions in some stores.

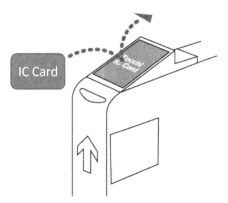

Fig. 5.   Automatic ticket gate.

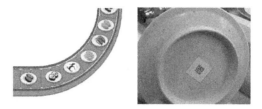

Fig. 6.   QR code for Belt-conveyor Sushi plate.

The T card issued at rental CD/DVD shop "TSUTAYA" can be used in many other stores such as gas stations and convenience stores for service points. This is one of the successful examples of BPN.

Geo-media and geo-service are also popular in Japan. Game characteristics inherent in SNS interchanges based on positional information are a key point. Suntory Holdings Ltd. collaborates with major bars and runs the "TRIS Highball" campaign (Suntory whisky and soda) through geo-service. This service is expected to develop into a new marketing tool.

3.3   *Examples of dining out and restaurants in Japan*

There is a McDonald's DS zone in Japan. Pokemon characters can be downloaded through an infrared network by those who carry Nintendo DS gaming machines into the McDonald's. The cost of feeding the family is a fixed cost. However, the variable cost of downloading Pokemon from the network is low even for many customers. Children come to McDonald's with their parents to get Pokemon characters and buy hamburgers and fries. This is a marketing model by McDonald's in collaboration with Nintendo.

Kura Corporation has many belt-conveyor sushi shops with the trademark, "additive-free Kura sushi" in Japan. Various kinds of sushi on a small plate are circulated on a conveyer belt along the customers' seats. The customer takes as many sushi plates as he/she likes. This is a cheap sushi shop of the half self-service type. Freshness management is performed by attaching a two-dimensional bar code (QR code) and an IC tag to the back of the plate, as shown in Fig. 6. Sushi plates on the conveyer for more than a specific amount of time are automatically disposed of. There is also an input port of used plates for every seat, and the number of used plates is calculated automatically. Then, the total for each seat is displayed through efficient accounting. This is a model for cost reduction, with the added value of "freshness".

4 Business Process Network

Nowadays, competitive advantage is not obtainable through the business model of one company only. It is necessary to build networks among companies.

4.1 *Competitive advantage in a value network*

When considering competitive advantage, it is important how a company achieves a functional (or process) prominent position in a value chain. At this time, the decision maker faces the problem of whether to buy a function (or process) or to develop a function as a strategy in order to secure competitive advantage. Generally, in industries in which environmental change is not much, the strategy of "developing a function" is used in a value chain to maintain long-term growth. However, when long-term growth is not expected, this strategy ends up raising costs. As a result, except for the core function (or process) in a value chain, the strategy of "buying a function" is becoming a popular method for obtaining a competitive advantage. In particular, in the IT industry, with its technical innovation and rapid changes in the market environment, these two strategies collide and the consequence is yet to be determined. The strategy of "buying a function" is successful in environment in which changes happen rapidly. However, the strategy of "developing a function" to correspond to rapid technical innovation has also been successful.

In today's IT industry, there are many companies that have improved price competitiveness by procuring parts at a low price from outside and then assembling them. However, one company is making profits through a new strategic effort. Panasonic Electric Works Co., Ltd, is maintaining a high rate of return through the strategy of "in-house parts production of plasma television by vertical integration of value chain", which is used to deal with everything within the company itself, from the parts to the finished goods. The in-house parts production rate of the plasma television of Panasonic is said to have reached 50%. The merits of in-house parts production are as follows: (1) preventing the external outflow of key parts with high functions has led to the maintenance of product price; (2) mass production parts increase sales volume by external sale, and their cost can be reduced; (3) change in design, new technology application, simultaneous global sale of a product, etc., become easy (*Nihon Keizai Shinbun*, July 27, 2006). On the other hand, the iPhone, which was put on the market in June 2007 and caused a sensation, is based on a different strategy from the independent management of Japanese companies. This strategy uses the power of parts suppliers to consider what a customer asks for and to realize the customer's demand. This strategy contrasts with the vertical integration of Panasonic.

The aforementioned examples show that the value network needs to focus on strategic problems rather than choose whether a company need to "buy a function" or "develop a function" in a value chain. Therefore, in this chapter, we provide a viewpoint on how companies choose business processes strategically in a value network. The strategic choice of functions (or processes) is also a problem in outsourcing business processes that exist inside the value network. Smith and Finger (2003, pp. 189–190) have provided the reasons for outsourcing business processes, as follows: (1) when the level of the process outcome cannot be expected to outweigh that of competitors, and (2) when the business process cannot contribute to differentiation or ensure a competitive advantage.

Today's competitive environment has already shifted from intercorporate competition to competition between syndicated value networks. With such an environmental change, business process network strategy that includes not only business process outsourcing but also business process collaboration has become an important way of securing a competitive advantage for a company. In other words, the business design of a value network is important. Bovet and Martha (2000, p. 2), who wrote a book named *Value Networks*, defined the value network as a business design that uses digital supply chain concepts to achieve both superior customer satisfaction and company profitability. In other words, in contrast to the traditional supply chain that manufactures products and pushes them through distribution channels in the hope that someone will buy them, a value network forms itself around its customers who are the center, as shown in Fig. 7. In a

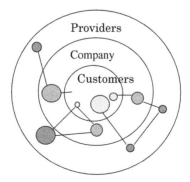

Fig. 7.   Value Network
Source: Bovet and Martha, 2000, p. 4.

value network, a company manages its network of providers to ensure rapid and cost-efficient fulfillment, although the customer–provider relationship is symbiotic, interactive, and value enhancing (Bovet and Martha, 2000, pp. 2–4). In the current ICT era, the business process network strategy of a value network is important because the relationship with the customer differs from that in the past, as shown in Fig. 7.

4.2 Collaboration of business process and virtual network organization

In today's intensely competitive, changeable environment, strategic effort that maintains and expands competitive advantage is necessary to reduce the risk of environmental change. This strategic effort identifies and cultivates core competences with limited management resources. In addition, for non-core processes, efforts that utilize external resources are necessary. This is because a company will be better able to reduce economic risk by using the properties of other companies than by creating or purchasing the required properties. Furthermore, the "flexibility of a company", or response to environmental change in a short period, can be created (Hagel, 2002).

In a business process network strategy, the design of the process collaboration among companies to secure competitive advantage is important. Kimura (2003, pp. 101–102) mentions the following two advantages of collaboration over competition:

(1) Superiority in creation of new competitive products and businesses.

Collaboration is an interactive activity in which economic units with outstanding core competences utilize each other's knowledge for knowledge creation. This knowledge creation is effective in the development of a new competitive product or business.
(2) Flexible and nimble alteration of the value chain and value system according to the change in the business environment.

In situations where customer's needs are diversified and change violently, requirements for the development and production of new products also change. It is not realistic for one company to have such competence. That is, collaboration with another company that has the required competence for new customer needs can save the development costs and time of a company.

On the other hand, the virtual network organization is often used as a form of the relationships among companies to promote process collaboration in a value network. In a virtual network organization, each company is connected in a network and outsources other processes, except for the process in which it is excellent. The network becomes an organization that acts as a single firm (Galbraith, 2002, pp. 161–162). This is a process collaboration strategy that maintains the best position by uniting the best process of a company with the best processes of other companies. The advantage of a virtual corporation is superiority in scale and range. This can be accomplished simultaneously through economies of scale and economies of range because the entire virtual corporation can act as a single firm even when it is not itself large scale. For example, although Benetton, the Italian fashion company, has entrusted most of its manufacturing to about 350 smaller companies, Benetton purchases all materials. As a result, Benetton is the world's largest company of woolen yarn purchase, and its remarkable position is established in the woolen yarn market (Galbraith, 2002, p. 163).

On the other hand, each company that belongs to a virtual corporation can either manage a particular field or play the role of a network integrator who unifies the whole business. Generally, the integrator company performs the following activities: (1) consider the customer important, (2) reduce outside suppliers, (3) boost superiority of scale, (4) unify the companies in the network, (5) influence the brand, and (6) provide an opportunity to beat competition (Galbraith, 2002, p. 167).

In today's business environment, it is said that processes are creatively destroyed and that process collaboration in a value network is effective because of the following reasons (Mizukoshi, 2003, p. 100): (1) the limits of previous business models accompanied by economic maturity, (2) globalization of competition in the business and consumers, (3) the present circumstances of deregulation, (4) development of an information network, and (5) new economical efficiency of the information due to the development of an information network.

5   Summary

We discuss several types of business models for the service industry and summarize some examples of ICT application in the business models of the Japanese service industry. We formulate a BPN framework with ICT. BPN is an effective technique that can be applied to many processes in various industries. Finally, the significance and effects of BPN are discussed with some examples from the service industry.

References

Bovet, D. and J. Martha, (2000). *Value Nets: Breaking the Supply Chain to Unlock Hidden Profits*, New York: Wiley.

Cho, T. (March 8, 2002). *Ideas about the Development of the Techno-Business Model*, Annual Conference of Society of Business Model (in Japanese) http://www006.upp.so-net.ne.JP/TTS.

David, F. R. (1999). *Concepts of Strategic Management*, 7th edn., Pearson Education.

Galbraith, J. R. (2002). *Designing Organizations: An Executive Guide to Strategy, Structure, and Process*, John Wiley & Sons (translation by Umezu, H. 2002. *Soshiki Sekkei no Kanri*, Tokyo: Seisansei-Syuppan, (in Japanese).

Honjo, T. (December 8, 1999). Obvious direction for business model patent, *Asahi* Newspaper (in Japanese).

Ishikawa, H. (2001). Limitation and effect of business model, *Journal of the Society of Office Automation*, 22(1), 45–51.

Hagel, J. III (2002). Leveraged growth: Expanding sales without sacrificing profits, *Harvard Business Review*, 80(10), 68–77.

Kimura, S. (2003). *Pattern of Relationship and Management Accounting*, Tokyo: Zeimukeirikyokai (in Japanese).

Looy, B. V, P. Gemmel and R. V. Dierdonck (2003). *Service Management and Integrated Approach*, London: Financial Times/Prentice Hall.

Magretta, J. (2002). Right definition of business model, *Diamond Harvard Business Review*, 8, 123–132.

Ministry of Economy, Trade and Industry (2007). *Approach of Innovation and Improvement of Productivity for Service Industry*, Research Institute of Economy, Tokyo: Trade and Industry (in Japanese).

Mizukoshi, Y. (2003). *Strategic Concepts of BCG: Principle of Competitive Advantage*, Tokyo: Diamond (in Japanese).

Naito, K. (2010). *Improvement of Productivity for Service Industry*, Tokyo: Nikkan-Kogyo Shinbunsya.

Nihon Keizai Shinbun (2006). TV Buhinnaiseikaga Koka, 27 July (In Japanese).

Shimomura, Y., T. Arai and T. Hara (2009). *Introduction of Service Engineering*, Tokyo: Tokyo University Publishing (in Japanese).

Smith, H. and P. Finger (2003). *Business Process Management: The Third Wave*, Florida: Meghan-Kiffer Press.

Teramoto,Y. and N. Iwasaki (2000). *Business Model Revolution*, Tokyo: Japan Productivity Center.

Index